"Jill has a great knack for using unique seasonings to make ordinary food taste great. I enjoyed everything I've tasted of her recipes. She has a chef-like quality to her recipes, but they are simple to make. I love feeling like I can actually cook something my children enjoy."

—Deanne Crockett

"All of my kids loved them. This book is a great idea. *Cap'n Crunch Chicken* came out really moist and crunchy."

—Gretchen Bartlett

"Jill has shared some of her recipes with my family and we found them to be full of flavor, easy to make, and something everyone enjoys. With seven in our family, that is not always easy to accomplish! I've made them for large crowds and everyone ALWAYS wants the recipes. They are simply that good!"

—Jana Dixon

"As a mother of young children, I feel a need to provide healthy food for my family. As a woman, I feel the need to be creative. By using these recipes from this amazing cookbook, I am able to make healthy, yummy food that my children will eat, while stretching my creativity beyond the pre-prepared foods that we have become accustomed to."

—Holly Davis

"My grandchildren have enjoyed the fun and creative recipes from this cookbook when they come to visit. It's a wonderful idea."

—Marty Ellis

A Second Helping of Praise . . .

"Our viewers love a Jill McKenzie recipe! She knows how to get kids to eat . . . without it being boring. She adds some unique twists to her recipes, creating the perfect combination of originality and taste. It's the perfect cookbook for getting your family back to the dinner table."

—Michelle Kettle,
Program Director, *Studio 5*,
Salt Lake City, Utah

"At Utah Valley University, our students are on tight schedules and usually work within tight budgets. Jill's fast, tasty, and inexpensive recipes are just what students are looking for. McKenzie is UVU's 'Hallway Gourmet,' and weekly brings gourmet delights to the campus halls and energetically engages students in learning how to prepare these simple but tasty foods. These homegrown recipes are fast and delectable, even when prepared by a novice like me."

—Grant Flygare, Director Office
of Student Involvement, Utah
Valley University, Orem, Utah

"Jill has created fun and nutritious meal ideas that will appeal to all the members of your family.

"I've had the opportunity to sample some of these recipes. They are savory and have time-saving ideas that will help you reclaim your mealtime together."

—Suzanne L. Price,
Pleasant Grove Macey's (retired),
Owner/Operator of Price Catering

52 WEEKS OF PROVEN RECIPES FOR PICKY KIDS

JILL McKENZIE

SHADOW
MOUNTAIN

To my wonderful, picky children,
Amber, Jessica, Joseph, Michael, Kaitee, and Jacob

Library of Congress Cataloging-in-Publication Data

McKenzie, Jill.
   52 weeks of proven recipes for picky kids / by Jill McKenzie.
      p.   cm.
  Includes index.
   ISBN 978-1-59038-986-7 (paperbound)
  1. Cookery.   I. Title.   II. Title: Fifty-two weeks of proven recipes for picky kids.
  TX652.M3685 2008
  641.5—dc22   2008018632

Printed in the United States of America
Worzalla Publishing Co., Stevens Point, WI

10   9   8   7   6   5   4   3   2   1

ACKNOWLEDGMENTS

Grateful thanks to Chris Schoebinger, an inspiring genius of good ideas; Jana Erickson, for letting this great idea incubate; Janna DeVore, for an amazing editing job; Lisa Mangum, Shauna Gibby, and Tonya Facemyer, and the rest of the Shadow Mountain team.

Thanks to the families who devoted their time and talents to prove and try these recipes; Suzanne at Macey's; Grant at UVU; and Michelle at KSL for adding to the momentum and joy of this project.

Thanks to Holly for last-minute details and encouragement.

Thanks to my dog, Sooner, who kept my feet warm while I was typing.

And, finally, special thanks to Roger, who is the pickiest of them all. I am so glad he picked me.

INTRODUCTION

"Is *this* what we're having for dinner? Yuck! Can I have some macaroni and cheese?" your child complains as you bring a lovingly prepared meal to the table, your back aching from standing in the kitchen for more than an hour and a stack of dirty pots and pans waiting in the sink. The only thing that could make the situation worse is your husband piping in with, "Or we could have hot dogs instead!"

This is a true story—it really happened to me; and I imagine that it happens in dozens of other homes in my neighborhood—and neighborhoods everywhere—on a nightly basis.

I wrote this book to help empower you to reclaim dinnertime in your home and to provide ideas, tools, and suggestions that can possibly obliterate dinnertime whining and complaining altogether, or at least reduce the complaints from nightly to monthly.

Before you dive into the recipes that follow, read through these tips. You may feel like you've gone back in time and are just introducing your baby to solid foods; but these tips really will make a difference in what your child—and husband, and even you—enjoy over time:

- It's better to take just one taste. Sometimes the threat of having to eat an entire portion is overwhelming. Promise yourself, or your child, that all that is needed is just a single bite. If, after trying a new food, you or your child insist that it's not going to be on the menu, then simply accept it.
- Be brave and introduce new foods more than once—even if it was rejected on the first try. Many of us have to try a food several times before developing a taste for it. Continue to offer a new food without force. Eventually you or your child just might acquire a taste for it.

1

- It's important to be a role model. Let your children see you enjoy a wide variety of foods. Just like you had to show your baby how to take his first bite of strained peaches, sometimes you need to show your eight-year-old that you, too, can eat vegetables. Scheduling family meals helps kids watch the adults in their family enjoying lots of different types of food. It also keeps a family healthier and happier when you eat together.
- Try foods in different forms. Your child may not like bananas, so try a smoothie with bananas and yogurt instead. Some foods that aren't so appealing in their natural state, can take on a whole new "a peel" in a different form.
- Be flexible, but disciplined. Don't snack on unhealthy foods between meals. When kids eat too many sweet treats, they are more likely to not be hungry at dinnertime and it will be easier for them to refuse to eat what you have prepared. Instead, when your children are hungry during the day, offer them healthy snacks like vegetable sticks or sliced fruit. If they are hungry enough, they will eat them. And when your children have been snacking on healthy foods, you can be flexible enough to occasionally let your kids skip eating a serving of vegetables at dinner because you know they have eaten them earlier in the day.
- Let dinner be a special time to focus on the family. Think of dinner as a chance for quality time rather than a chance to focus on the food your child won't eat. Put less pressure on eating and more emphasis on sharing the details of the day.
- Let the children get involved in the preparation of dinner. Not only will you have fun; but you can almost count on children eating what they have prepared.

Many of us come from a generation of quick-and-easy meals, so that's what we are used to. But too often, those straight-from-the-can or packaged dinners are lacking in nutrition and taste. But we can have both. This book is designed to introduce your kids to new foods, with new ideas for making flavorful dishes that are fun, easy to make, and packed full of real nutrition for real families. Each week of the year, try a new meal from the recipes in this book and see if dinnertime whining turns into dinnertime joy as your family comes to the table. Enjoy!

PANTRY AND FREEZER ESSENTIALS

As part of your adventure in reclaiming your family dinnertime, here is a handy list of pantry-friendly ingredients that are useful to have on-hand.

CANNED GOODS

10.75-ounce cans of cream of chicken soup

10.75-ounce cans of cream of mushroom soup

10-ounce cans of mild enchilada sauce

14,5-ounce cans of diced tomatoes

14-ounce cans of coconut milk

15-ounce cans of black beans

20-ounce cans of fruit cocktail

20-ounce cans of pineapple chunks or tidbits

20-ounce jars of Alfredo sauce

20-ounce jars of spaghetti sauce

8-ounce cans of mandarin oranges

Jar of minced garlic

DRY GOODS

10-inch flour tortillas

Bread crumbs

Brownie mixes

Long-grain white or brown rice

Oreo® cookies

Pasta (shells, wagon wheel, fettuccini, spaghetti)

Pecan gems

Ritz® crackers

Tortilla chip strips

Walnut gems

FREEZER ITEMS

10-ounce bags of spinach
16-ounce bags of raspberries
Lemonade concentrate
Orange juice concentrate
Rhodes® frozen rolls

LIQUIDS

14-ounce cans of chicken broth
Barbecue sauce
Coca-Cola® or Sprite®
Ketchup
Lemon juice
Lime juice
Mayonnaise
Rice vinegar
Vanilla extract
Worcestershire sauce

MIXES

Chicken gravy mix packets
Hidden Valley Buttermilk Ranch®
    packet
Hidden Valley Fiesta Ranch Dip®
    spice packet
Instant pudding mixes (chocolate,
    coconut)

SPICES

Allspice
Basil
Black pepper
Chili powder
Chives
Cumin
Dry mustard
Garlic salt
Ground cloves
Nutmeg
Oregano
Salt
Seasoned salt
Sesame seeds

Week 1

Lasagna is one food that many kids actually love. This is a super easy version of the dish. You may consider pureeing a few carrots or some zucchini to stir into the sauce. The kids won't know it's there; and you'll feel good knowing they got some veggies in. Served with Parmesan Texas Rolls and chocolaty Mud Slides for dessert, this meal is sure to please your picky eaters.

Easy Skillet Lasagna

    3   cups your favorite dried pasta
    1   pound lean ground beef
    1   26-ounce jar pasta sauce
    1½ cups grated mozzarella cheese
    ¼   cup grated Parmesan cheese

COOK PASTA ACCORDING TO PACKAGE DIRECTIONS; drain. Meanwhile, cook meat in a medium sized skillet until browned; drain off fat and remove to a bowl or platter. Wipe skillet with a paper towel. Spread half of cooked pasta in skillet. Cover with half of the sauce. Spoon meat over sauce and sprinkle with 1 cup of the mozzarella cheese. Top with remaining pasta and sauce. Sprinkle remaining cheese on top. Cook, covered, over medium heat for 5 to 7 minutes. Remove from heat and let stand 1 minute. Serve.

Serves 6.

Parmesan Texas Rolls

    1   bag frozen Rhodes® Texas Rolls, white or whole wheat
    1   tablespoon parsley flakes
    1½ cups grated Parmesan cheese
    1   teaspoon garlic powder
    ½   cup butter, melted

Place 12 frozen rolls on a plate and microwave on high power for 2 minutes. Repeat with remaining 12 rolls. In a small bowl, combine parsley flakes, Parmesan cheese, and garlic powder. Put melted butter in a separate bowl. Take the pliable but cool rolls and roll them in the butter then the Parmesan mixture. Place rolls on a greased cookie sheet and let rise for 45 minutes to an hour. Bake at 325 degrees for 15 to 20 minutes, until golden brown.

Makes 24 rolls.

Mud Slides

4	cups cold milk
2	3-ounce packages chocolate-flavored instant pudding
28	chocolate sandwich cookies, finely crushed, about 3 cups
4	cups Cool Whip®, thawed

Pour milk into a 1-quart container with a tight-fitting lid. Add pudding mix, cover tightly, and shake vigorously at least 45 seconds; pour evenly into 6 glasses. Gently stir 2 cups of the cookie crumbs into whipped topping until blended. Spoon evenly over pudding in glasses; sprinkle with remaining cookie crumbs.

Refrigerate until ready to serve.

Serves 6.

You can also chill the pudding in glasses that have been set at a 45-degree angle in the refrigerator for a true mudslide effect.

Week 2

Sometimes, the only thing you want to eat is chips and dip. This week, try a great recipe to meet that need, balanced with a delightful and refreshing fruit salad. Or, serve a simple green salad topped with my tomatillo dressing (see Week 4) and accompanied by tortilla chips served with guacamole and pico de gallo.

Mexican Delicioso

2	16-ounce cans refried beans
4	large, ripe avocados
1	tablespoon lemon juice
1	teaspoon ground cumin
1	teaspoon chili powder
1	teaspoon seasoned salt
½	teaspoon garlic powder or 1 clove fresh garlic, minced
1	16-ounce carton sour cream
1	1.25-ounce packet taco seasoning
1	large tomato, chopped
2	cups shredded sharp cheddar cheese
1	2.25-ounce can chopped olives
½	cup sliced green onions or 1 small yellow onion, chopped
½ to 1	cup chopped, fresh cilantro leaves
	Tortilla chips

SPREAD REFRIED BEANS ON TWO SERVING PLATTERS or in a 9x13-inch baking dish. Peel and pit avocados. In a medium bowl mash the avocados. Stir in the lemon juice, cumin, chili powder, seasoned salt, and garlic. Spread avocado mixture over the beans with a rubber spatula. In another medium bowl, combine sour cream and taco seasoning. Spread over avocado layer.

Top with tomatoes, cheese, olives, onions, and cilantro. Serve with tortilla chips.

Serves 6 to 8.

SWEET AMBROSIA

1   cup red seedless grapes
1   cup green seedless grapes
1   cup black seedless grapes
2   cups sliced bananas
1   20-ounce can pineapple tidbits or half of a fresh pineapple, sliced into tidbits
1   cup sliced strawberries
3   tablespoons lemon juice
3   tablespoons honey

COMBINE FRUIT IN A LARGE BOWL. In a separate, smaller bowl, mix lemon juice and honey and pour over fruit. Serve immediately.

Serves 4 to 6.

PICO DE GALLO

3   fresh tomatoes, finely chopped
1   onion, finely chopped
1   green pepper, finely chopped
1   4.5-ounce can mild green chilies
1   handful chopped, fresh cilantro leaves
2   teaspoons seasoned salt
1   teaspoon ground cumin
2   teaspoons chopped garlic
1   teaspoon dried basil

1   teaspoon dried oregano
2   tablespoons lime juice, fresh or bottled

COMBINE ALL INGREDIENTS IN A SMALL BOWL. Chill until ready to serve.
Makes 2 cups.

GUACAMOLE

3   ripe avocados, peeled and mashed in a bowl
2   tablespoons lime juice, fresh or bottled
1   teaspoon seasoned salt
1   teaspoon minced garlic
1   teaspoon ground cumin
3   teaspoons chopped, fresh cilantro leaves

COMBINE ALL INGREDIENTS IN A SMALL BOWL. Chill until served.
Makes 1½ cups.

WEEK 3

For a satisfying dinner that everyone likes and that is also fun to eat, serve the following recipes. Instead of utensils, use chopsticks and ask your kids to find out if it's really possible to eat rice with chopsticks. (If it turns out it's not, fingers will do nicely too!)

LETTUCE WRAPS

12	large leaves iceberg lettuce, washed and patted dry
2	tablespoons sesame oil
1	small onion, chopped
1	clove garlic, finely chopped
1	pound ground pork, chicken, turkey, or beef (your choice)
1	cup cashews
1	cup salted peanuts
1	cup Craisins®
1	6.75-ounce package crunchy rice noodles or 1 package dry ramen noodles, crushed

Sauce

5	tablespoons soy sauce
1	tablespoon sugar
	Juice of 2 limes
1	tablespoon cornstarch
1	tablespoon water
½	cup orange juice, prepared from concentrate

MAKE SURE LETTUCE LEAVES ARE WASHED AND PATTED dry with paper towels; set aside. Heat sesame oil over medium heat in a large skillet. Add onions and garlic and sauté for just a few minutes. This will season the oil and the pan. Add ground meat and cook thoroughly; set aside. In a separate bowl, whisk together sauce ingredients. Pour over meat mixture and bring to a boil over medium-high heat. The sauce will thicken slightly. Stir in the cashews, peanuts, and Craisins. Let mixture steam for about 4 minutes. Serve on a bed of crushed rice noodles or ramen. Individual eaters will spoon mixture into center of lettuce and wrap up like a burrito. Serve with soy sauce, or, if you're really adventurous, hot Chinese mustard.

Serves 6 to 8.

EGG DROP SOUP

1 tablespoon vegetable oil
3 cloves garlic, crushed
1 teaspoon freshly grated ginger, or chopped ginger
3 cups chicken stock, or 2 14-ounce cans chicken broth
1 14.75-ounce can cream-style corn*
1 egg
Salt and pepper, to taste
Chopped fresh cilantro leaves, for garnishing
Paprika, for garnishing
Soy sauce

HEAT THE OIL IN A LARGE SAUCEPAN OVER MEDIUM HEAT. Add garlic and sauté for 1 minute, stirring constantly. Stir in ginger, chicken stock, and cream-style corn. Bring mixture to a boil. Salt and pepper to taste. Return soup to a boil. Beat the egg, then gently pour it into the soup so it forms long strands. Simmer gently for about 30 seconds until just set. Ladle the soup into bowls and serve hot, garnished with chopped cilantro and a sprinkling of paprika. If desired, add a dash of soy sauce to heighten the taste.

Serves 4 to 6.

If children have a difficult time eating chunks of corn, blend the can of cream-style corn in a blender until smooth and creamy, then add to soup.

WEEK 4

This week's recipes are flavorful and fun—just what you need in the middle of the winter doldrums. Most of the recipes can be made ahead and/or frozen for a quick meal down the road. They are also very versatile and can be served over rice, on their own, or as a delicious layered dish (coupled with recipes from Week 2) in individual pie tins—a sure hit with kids. Leftovers are perfect for use in burritos, enchiladas, tacos, or sandwiches.

BAJA BONANZA CILANTRO CHICKEN

2	pounds frozen chicken breasts
2	14-ounce cans chicken broth
1	lime, cut into wedges
1	handful chopped, fresh cilantro leaves
1	tablespoon chopped garlic
1	teaspoon dry mustard
1	teaspoon ground cumin
1	teaspoon chili powder
2	teaspoons seasoned salt

PLACE THE FROZEN CHICKEN AND CHICKEN BROTH in the bottom of a 4-quart slow cooker. Squeeze lime juice over the chicken. Discard all but 2 of the wedges; place those in with the chicken. Add remaining ingredients and stir. Simmer for approximately 8 hours on low heat. When the chicken is done, take 2 forks and shred the chicken. Keep in the slow cooker and serve in natural juices over rice or as part of another dish. Freeze leftover chicken to use in burritos, tacos, enchiladas, or to make a great chicken sandwich.

Serves 6 to 8.

SWEET RICE

2   tablespoons olive oil
4   cups long-grain brown or white rice
1   yellow Walla Walla onion, chopped
1   tablespoon lime juice
1   tablespoon ground cumin
1   teaspoon dried basil
1   14-ounce can coconut milk
½   cup frozen orange juice concentrate
1   handful fresh, chopped cilantro leaves
6   cups water or chicken broth

HEAT OIL IN A LARGE SAUCEPAN OVER MEDIUM HEAT. Add rice, onions, lime juice, cumin, and basil and sauté until rice is lightly browned. Add the rest of the ingredients. Stir. Bring to a boil for 2 minutes, cover with a lid, and reduce heat. Simmer for 20 minutes. This is a great side dish or filling for enchiladas, tacos, and burritos.

Serves 6 to 8.

PORK BARBACOA

1   2-pound pork roast
3   12-ounce cans Coca-Cola® or Sprite®
1   14-ounce can chicken broth
1   cup brown sugar, packed
2   tablespoons butter
1   20-ounce can pineapple chunks, undrained
1   tablespoon ground cumin
2   teaspoons seasoned salt

1   cup ketchup
2   tablespoons red wine vinegar

Place pork roast in a large, nonreactive bowl. Pour soda over the top, cover with plastic wrap and marinate in the refrigerator for at least 3 hours, or overnight. In a 4-quart slow cooker, combine chicken broth, brown sugar, butter, pineapple chunks (including juice), cumin, seasoned salt, ketchup, and vinegar. Discard soda marinade and place pork roast in the slow cooker. Simmer on low for at least 8 hours. Shred pork with 2 forks and serve in sweetened natural juices over rice or as part of another dish.

Serves 10 to 12.

Dinner in Pie Tins

6 to 8   10-inch flour tortillas
1   recipe Sweet Rice or Baja Beans (see recipes on pages 13 and 75)
1   bag salad greens
1   recipe Baja Bonanza Cilantro Chicken or Pork Barbacoa (see recipes on pages 12 and 13)
    Guacamole (see recipe on page 9)
    Pico de Gallo (see recipe on page 8)
2   cups shredded cheddar cheese
    Sour cream
1   recipe Jill's Tomatillo Dressing (see recipe on page 15)
    Tortilla chips, crushed
    Pie tins for each family member

In each pie tin, let family members layer ingredients in this order (using as many or as few ingredients as each person likes): tortilla, beans or rice, salad greens, chicken or pork, guacamole, pico de gallo, cheese, sour cream, Jill's Tomatillo Dressing, crushed tortilla chips.

Serves 6 to 8.

Jill's Tomatillo Dressing

6	tomatillos
½	.87-ounce packet buttermilk ranch dressing
1	1.1-ounce packet Hidden Valley Fiesta Ranch Dip®
1	cup chopped, fresh cilantro leaves
2	tablespoons chopped garlic
½	cup lime juice
1	cup buttermilk
1	cup mayonnaise
½	cup milk

PEEL HUSKS OFF TOMATILLOS AND DISCARD. Wash tomatillos and place in blender along with all remaining ingredients. Blend until a fine sauce forms. Chill until ready to serve.

Makes 2 cups.

Week 5

I grew up in Pingree, Idaho, where spuds were everywhere. This week's main dish includes spuds and is one of my favorites. It's the perfect embodiment of an Idaho dinner: comforting, down-home goodness!

Idaho Dinner

2   cups cooked, cubed ham
1   32-ounce package shredded frozen potatoes
1   10.75-ounce can cream of mushroom soup
2   cups sour cream
2   cups heavy cream
½   cup chopped onion
2   tablespoons butter
1   tube Ritz® crackers (4 tubes come in a box), crushed
1   cup shredded cheddar cheese

PREHEAT OVEN TO 350 DEGREES. Combine ham, frozen shredded potatoes, soup, sour cream, cream, and onion in a large bowl. Pour into a 9x13-inch baking dish. Melt 2 tablespoons butter in a small skillet over medium heat. Add crushed crackers and sauté until toasted. Sprinkle the cheese and then the crackers on top of the casserole. Bake for 45 minutes.

Serves 6.

TREES AND CHEESE

1   head of broccoli, or 1 10-ounce package frozen broccoli florets
1   10.75-ounce can Campbell's® Condensed Cheddar Cheese Soup

PLACE THE FLORETS OF BROCCOLI IN A MEDIUM-SIZED, microwaveable bowl. Pour ½-inch water in the bowl. Pour cheese soup over the top of the broccoli and cover bowl with plastic wrap. Microwave on high for 4 minutes. Serve hot.

Serves 6.

COCONUT CREAM SALAD*

2   cups buttermilk
2   3-ounce packages instant coconut cream pudding
1   16-ounce large tub Cool Whip®, thawed
2   20-ounce cans tropical fruit cocktail, drained
2   8-ounce cans mandarin oranges, drained
2   20-ounce cans pineapple tidbits, drained

IN A LARGE BOWL, STIR BUTTERMILK AND DRY PUDDING mixes together. Fold in Cool Whip, followed by the well-drained fruits. Chill 24 hours before serving.

Serves 6.

Prepare this recipe a day in advance of serving.

WEEK 6

Squash is a wonderful vegetable and full of so many vitamins. It can, however, be a difficult vegetable to get children to eat. My children felt that way, so I experimented with some ideas and came up with a very tasty sauce that goes over any pasta. Try it this week, and then pat yourself on the back for getting your kids to eat their veggies!

SQUASHED BUTTERNUT SAUCE AND PASTA

1   cup butter
1   tablespoon minced garlic
1   tablespoon salt
1   teaspoon ground black pepper
1   teaspoon dill seed
1   2-pound butternut squash, peeled and diced
5   cubes chicken bouillon dissolved in 3 cups water, or 2 14-ounce cans chicken broth
2   cups heavy cream
1   teaspoon ground cloves
1   teaspoon ground allspice
1   teaspoon ground nutmeg
1   pound dry pasta, cooked according to package directions

MELT BUTTER IN LARGE SAUCEPAN OVER MEDIUM HEAT. Stir in garlic, salt, pepper, and dill seed. Add butternut squash and stir. Reduce heat to medium-low and simmer for about 15 minutes, until squash is very tender. Pour squash mixture into a blender and blend until pureed. Pour sauce back into saucepan. Add chicken broth, heavy cream, ground cloves, allspice, and nutmeg. Stir and simmer to blend the spices. If consistency is thin, mix 3 tablespoons flour with 3 tablespoons water, stir into the sauce, and then bring to a rolling boil, stirring constantly, to thicken. Serve atop your family's favorite cooked pasta.

Serves 6 to 12.

Frozen Fruit Salad

1   8-ounce package cream cheese, softened
¾   cup sugar
1   12-ounce tub Cool Whip®, thawed
2   bananas, diced
1   20-ounce can pineapple tidbits, drained
1   16-ounce package frozen raspberries, drained

Beat cream cheese and sugar with an electric mixer until smooth and creamy. Fold in Cool Whip and add remaining ingredients. Line a 8½x4½ glass or metal bread pan with waxed paper. Pour in fruit mixture and freeze. When ready to serve, dunk bottom of bread pan in a bowl of warm water for a few seconds, then turn onto plate and slice. Your children will think you are giving them ice cream for dinner.

Serves 6.

Green Beans with Butter and Bacon

⅓   cup butter
2   14.5-ounce cans green beans, drained, or 1 pound fresh green beans, snipped, washed, and steamed until tender
½   pound bacon, cooked crisp and crumbled

Put butter and beans in a medium saucepan and warm over medium-low heat until butter melts. Stir in crumbled bacon and serve hot.

Serves 6.

WEEK 7

This week, go vegetarian! Tell the kids that some people who are vegetarians eat this way every day. It is definitely an alternative and healthy way to eat. Then you can spoil them with dessert.

VEGETARIAN ENCHILADAS

2 10-ounce cans mild enchilada sauce
2 cups heavy cream, divided
2 tablespoons olive oil
1 large yellow onion, chopped
1 red bell pepper, cleaned and chopped
4 teaspoons chopped garlic
1 8-ounce package fresh baby portabella mushrooms, finely chopped
1 6-ounce package fresh baby spinach, finely chopped
1 handful chopped, fresh cilantro leaves, divided
1 4.5-ounce can green chilies
1 tablespoon seasoned salt
1 tablespoon chili powder
1 teaspoon dried oregano
1 teaspoon dried basil
1 teaspoon cumin
3 cups shredded mozzarella cheese, divided
1 cup crumbled Mexican queso fresca (fresh Mexican cheese)
2 cups shredded cheddar cheese
20 10-inch flour tortillas
1 tomato, chopped

HEAT OVEN TO 350 DEGREES. Coat a 9x13-inch glass pan or baking dish with nonstick cooking spray.

In a medium saucepan, warm enchilada sauce and 1½ cups of the cream over medium heat for about 3 minutes, stirring occasionally until heated through; set aside.

In a large skillet, heat olive oil over medium heat. Add onion, red bell pepper, and garlic. Cook until onion and peppers are tender. Stir in the mushrooms; cook for about 7 minutes, stirring occasionally, until tender. Transfer vegetable mixture to food processor or blender. Add spinach, ½ of the cilantro, green chilies, seasoned salt, chili powder, oregano, basil, cumin, and remaining ½ cup cream. Pulse 5 times until mushrooms and spinach are coarsely chopped. Pour mixture into a large bowl. Stir in 2 cups of the mozzarella cheese and the crumbled Mexican cheese. Spoon ½ cup of the warmed enchilada-cream sauce into prepared pan and spread evenly to coat bottom. Spoon ⅓ cup of the vegetable filling down center of each tortilla. Roll up tortillas; place seam sides down on sauce in baking dish. Pour remaining sauce evenly over tortillas; sprinkle with remaining cheeses. Spray a sheet of aluminum foil with nonstick cooking spray and cover enchiladas. Bake for 40 minutes. Sprinkle with remaining cilantro and fresh tomato before serving.

Serves 6 to 8.

CREAMY LEMON DELIGHT

3   eggs
¾   cup frozen lemonade concentrate, thawed
3   teaspoons lemon zest
2   teaspoons vanilla extract
2   8-ounce packages cream cheese, softened
6   lemon slices, for garnish
6   cream-filled vanilla cookies

CRACK EGGS INTO A MEDIUM SAUCEPAN and beat well with a fork. Add lemon concentrate and mix well. Cook and stir over low heat for 8 to 10 minutes or until mixture is thickened and reaches 160 degrees. Cool to room temperature. Stir in lemon zest and vanilla extract. In a medium mixing bowl, beat cream cheese and lemon mixture until well blended. Spoon into dessert dishes and refrigerate until chilled. Top with lemon slices and cream-filled cookies and serve.

Serves 6.

WEEK 8

This week's meals are both budget friendly and kid friendly. Let the kids help you assemble the ice cream sandwiches before dinner. Freeze them until it's time to for dessert—and tell the kids that eating their creations comes with the stipulation that the rest of the dinner was tasted!

BUDGET MINUTE STEAKS

¾ cup all-purpose flour
1 teaspoon ground black pepper
2 teaspoons garlic salt
6 5-ounce beef cube steaks
2 tablespoons canola oil
1 cup ketchup
3 tablespoons lemon juice
3 teaspoons Worcestershire sauce
2 teaspoons dry mustard

IN A LARGE ZIPLOC BAG, COMBINE FLOUR, PEPPER, and garlic salt. Add the steaks, one at a time, and shake to coat. Heat oil in a large skillet over medium heat. Add steaks and cook for 3 to 4 minutes on each side or until no longer pink. Remove and keep warm. Stir remaining ingredients into the skillet to create a yummy sauce. Heat until warm and bubbly. Serve sauce atop the steaks or pass for dipping.

Serves 6.

Parmesan Peas and Rice

4   tablespoons butter
2   cups long grain rice
3   green onions, chopped
1   tablespoon seasoned salt
1   teaspoon ground black pepper
4   cups chicken broth
2   cups frozen peas
¾   cup grated Parmesan cheese

Melt butter in a large saucepan over medium heat. Add rice, onions, salt, and pepper and sauté until rice is browned and onions are tender. Stir in broth and bring to a boil over high heat. Reduce heat, cover, and simmer for 10 minutes. Add peas; cover and cook 5 to 6 more minutes until liquid is absorbed and rice is tender. Stir in Parmesan cheese. Serve hot.

Serves 6.

Delightful Brownie Ice Cream Sandwiches

1   15.5-ounce box Duncan Hines® Milk Chocolate Chunk brownie mix
¼   cup all-purpose flour
½   cup butter, melted
1   egg
1   teaspoon vanilla
1   quart vanilla ice cream, or your favorite flavor

Preheat oven to 375 degrees. In a large bowl, stir together brownie mix and flour. Add butter, egg, and vanilla; stir until blended. Let dough stand

15 minutes for easier handling. Shape dough into 24 1½-inch balls. Dough will be soft. Place 2 inches apart on ungreased large cookie sheet. Bake 10 to 13 minutes or until set and tops appear dry. Cool on cookie sheet 1 minute; remove from cookie sheet to cooling rack. Cool completely, for about 30 minutes. Set out ice cream to soften about 5 or 10 minutes into cooling time.

Spoon 1 scoop of ice cream between 2 cookies to create a sandwich. Cut waxed paper into 4-inch squares and place on either side of cookie sandwich. Place in a plastic bag and freeze. Repeat for remaining cookies.

Makes 12 ice cream sandwiches.

WEEK 9

Pasta and garlic bread are a staple in most homes with picky eaters. This week, try a new recipe that doesn't involve cooking spaghetti noodles and dumping a can of sauce on top. Let the kids help you stuff the shells and sprinkle the cheese over the top. Extend the "cheesy" theme and add shredded cheddar cheese to your garlic bread. After all, what kid doesn't love gooey, melted cheese?

CHEESY STUFFED SHELLS

24   uncooked jumbo pasta shells
3   cups shredded mozzarella cheese, divided
1   cup shredded asiago cheese
1   cup ricotta cheese
1   cup cottage cheese
4   tablespoons minced chives
1   10-ounce package frozen chopped spinach, thawed and squeezed dry
4   cups meatless spaghetti sauce, divided

PREHEAT OVEN TO 350 DEGREES. Cook pasta according to package directions. In a small bowl, combine half the mozzarella cheese, asiago cheese, ricotta cheese, cottage cheese, chives, and 1 cup of the spinach. (Save remaining spinach for other uses.) Spread 2 cups of the spaghetti sauce into a shallow 9x13-inch glass baking dish coated with cooking spray. Drain pasta; stuff shells with cheese mixture and arrange in baking dish. Top with remaining spaghetti sauce and mozzarella. Bake 30 minutes.

Serves 4 to 6.

CHEESY GARLIC BREAD

1 large loaf French bread
½ cup butter, softened
1 teaspoon seasoned salt
1 teaspoon garlic powder
1 cup shredded cheddar cheese

PREHEAT OVEN TO 350 DEGREES. Cut French bread in half length-wise. Spread butter onto soft sides of cut French bread. Sprinkle seasoned salt, garlic powder, and cheese onto bread. Bake 5 to 10 minutes, until cheese is melted and bread is lightly toasted. Cut into squares and serve immediately.

Serves 6 to 8.

WEEK 10

This week, put some variety in your menu with these exciting but easy-to-make dishes. Let your kids in on the act by having them fold the dumplings. They can make different shapes and talk about their day as you work together. When mealtime comes, it's almost a given that they'll want to dig right into their creations.

DUMPLINGS

1   pound ground pork
2   tablespoons freshly grated ginger
1   16-ounce package chopped cabbage with carrots
2   tablespoons rice vinegar, divided
2   tablespoons soy sauce, divided
4   tablespoons sesame oil, divided
1   teaspoon salt
1   teaspoon ground black pepper
1   package Azumaya® Square Wraps
1   cup warm water

COOK PORK IN A LARGE SKILLET OVER MEDIUM heat until browned and crispy. In a large mixing bowl, combine browned pork, ginger, chopped cabbage with carrots, 1 tablespoon rice vinegar, 1 tablespoon soy sauce, 1 tablespoon sesame oil, salt, and pepper.

Working a wrap at a time, place a spoonful of stuffing in the center of the square. Wet a finger in the warm cup of water and moisten all edges of the square wrap. Fold each wrap over, pressing the edges together tightly to seal. Arrange on a plate or cookie sheet and store in the refrigerator until you are ready to cook the dumplings. You can cook the dumplings one of two ways, boiling or frying.

To boil the dumplings, carefully add them to a large pot of hot water; bring water to a boil. Boil for 2 minutes. Remove dumplings to a plate or strainer.

To fry dumplings, heat 1 inch of vegetable oil in a large skillet over medium-high heat. Carefully add dumplings to hot oil. After 1 or 2 minutes, turn dumplings over with long tongs. Cook another minute, and then remove dumplings to a paper-towel lined plate. The paper towels will soak up some of the oil.

While dumplings cool slightly, prepare a dipping sauce by mixing the remaining rice vinegar, soy sauce, and sesame oil in a small bowl.

Serves 6 to 8.

SESAME NOODLES WITH PORK AND CILANTRO

1	clove garlic, chopped
1	scallion, chopped
1	handful finely chopped, fresh cilantro leaves
1	10.5-ounce package fine egg noodles
2	tablespoons vegetable oil
2	teaspoons sesame oil
1½	cups pre-cooked pork, cut into cubes
2	tablespoons lime juice
1	teaspoon sesame seeds, toasted

PUREE GARLIC, SCALLION, AND CILANTRO IN A BLENDER to form a smooth paste; set aside. Bring 4 quarts water to a boil in a large pot. Drop the noodles into the boiling water; return to a boil and simmer for 4 minutes or according to package directions. Meanwhile, heat the oil in a wok or frying pan over medium heat. Stir in the pureed cilantro mixture. Cook, stirring, for

1 minute. Stir in the pork and stir-fry for 2 minutes. Add lime juice and cook for an additional minute. Drain noodles and toss the into the wok with the other ingredients. Sprinkle with toasted sesame seeds and serve.

Serves 4 to 6.

WEEK 11

This week's main dish has down-home warmth and great versatility. Moms can throw in anything to change the texture or add nutritional value. Sneaky moms can even puree zucchini, squash, or carrots to add to the sauce. Your kids won't even realize that they've eaten their veggies for the night! And the Cheesy Stix are certain to please—and surprise—all of your picky eaters.

TOMATO PASTA DELUXE

- 2 pounds multicolored wagon wheel pasta
- 2 tablespoons olive oil
- 1 small onion, diced
- 2 cloves garlic, minced
- 1 14.5-ounce can diced tomatoes with green chilies
- 1 teaspoon garlic salt
- 2 teaspoons salt
- 1 tablespoon chili powder
- 1 40-ounce jar Ragu® tomato sauce
- 2 cups cream
- 1 teaspoon dried or 1 tablespoon fresh oregano
- 1 teaspoon dried or 1 tablespoon fresh basil
- 2 cups grated Parmesan or mozzarella cheese

PREPARE PASTA ACCORDING TO DIRECTIONS. While pasta is cooking, heat oil in a large saucepan over medium heat. Sauté onions, minced garlic, diced tomatoes with green chilies, salts, and chili powder for 3 minutes. Stir in the Ragu, cream, oregano, and basil and bring to a slow rolling boil for 3 minutes; reduce heat and simmer an additional 10 minutes. Drain pasta and pour sauce over the top; let the children top it off with cheese. Enjoy!

Serves 6 to 8.

CHEESY STIX

3 eggs
1 cup fine dry bread crumbs
½ cup all-purpose flour
½ teaspoon garlic powder
½ teaspoon ground cumin
½ teaspoon dried oregano leaves
⅛ teaspoon salt
⅛ teaspoon ground black pepper
2 8-ounce packages mozzarella cheese sticks*
   Vegetable oil
2 cups ranch salad dressing

IN A SHALLOW DISH, BEAT EGGS; SET ASIDE. In another shallow dish, combine bread crumbs, flour, garlic powder, cumin, oregano, salt, and pepper. Dip cheese sticks in beaten eggs and then coat with crumb mixture.

In a large skillet heat 1 inch of oil to about 365 degrees. Fry coated cheese sticks, a few at a time, in hot oil for 1 to 2 minutes until golden brown, turning once. Drain on paper towels and serve with ranch dressing.

Serves 6 to 8.

You can also cut a 16-ounce block of mozzarella cheese into sticks.

FROZEN WALDORF SALAD

1	9-ounce can crushed pineapple
2	eggs, slightly beaten
½	cup sugar
¼	cup lemon juice
⅛	teaspoon salt
¼	cup mayonnaise
2½	cups diced apples
1	cup sliced strawberries
½	cup chopped pecans or walnut gems
⅓	cup miniature marshmallows
½	cup heavy cream, chilled

DRAIN PINEAPPLE, RESERVING JUICE, AND SET ASIDE. In a small saucepan, combine eggs, sugar, lemon juice, salt, and reserved pineapple juice. Cook over low heat, stirring constantly, until slightly thickened, about 20 minutes. Remove from heat and let cool. Fold in mayonnaise. In a large bowl, combine drained pineapple, apples, strawberries, nuts, and marshmallows. In a separate bowl, whip cream; fold into cooled egg mixture. Pour over fruit mixture and toss to mix. Fill a 6-cup mold or bowl and freeze firm, about 3 to 4 hours.

Serves 6 to 8.

WEEK 12

Anytime can be a great time for breakfast. This week, turn the tables on dinner and serve up a delicious breakfast for the evening meal. And check out the dessert! These chocolate crepes are simply heaven. Picky eaters might not like the filling, but nothing will stop them from eating a rolled-up chocolate crepe topped with caramel sauce-whipped cream.

MULTIGRAIN BREAKFAST OR ANYTIME MUFFINS

1	cup 10-grain hot cereal, such as Bob's Red Mill®
1¼	cup buttermilk*
½	cup sugar
1	egg
⅓	cup butter
1	teaspoon baking powder
1	teaspoon baking soda
1	teaspoon salt
1	cup all-purpose flour

PREHEAT OVEN TO 400 DEGREES. Grease a standard muffin pan, or line with 12 paper cups.

In a medium bowl, combine the 10-grain cereal and buttermilk and let stand for 10 minutes. In a separate bowl, cream sugar, egg, and butter together until light and fluffy. Add dry ingredients and milk mixture to creamed mixture. Stir only until just mixed. Spoon into greased muffin pan. Bake for 15 minutes.

Makes 12 muffins.

Heavy cream or milk can be used in place of the buttermilk, if desired.

QUICK AND FRUITY CRESCENT WAFFLES

¼ cup pecan pieces

1 8-ounce can refrigerated crescent rolls

½ cup fresh or frozen blueberries, or your favorite berries

1 6-ounce carton blueberry yogurt, or your favorite berry-flavored yogurt

1 firm, ripe banana, cut into ¼-inch slices

1 cup raspberries

1 cup strawberries, sliced

½ cup whipped cream or Cool Whip®

¼ teaspoon ground cinnamon (optional)

PREHEAT OVEN TO 200 DEGREES. Spray waffle maker with nonstick cooking spray and preheat.

Toast pecans in a nonstick skillet over medium heat for 5 to 7 minutes, stirring frequently, until lightly browned. Remove from skillet and set aside. Separate crescent dough into 8 triangles. Place 2 or 3 triangles at a time on waffle iron. Cook 1 to 2 minutes or until golden brown. Place cooked waffles on cookie sheet in oven to keep warm. In a medium saucepan, heat blueberries and yogurt over medium heat, stirring occasionally, until hot. To serve, stack 2 crescent waffles, slightly overlapping, on each serving plate. Spoon hot fruit sauce over the top, then top with banana slices, nuts, and raspberries and strawberries (or any other of your favorite berries). Add a dollop of whipped cream to the top and, if desired, sprinkle with cinnamon. Enjoy!

Serves 4 to 6.

BANANA-FILLED CHOCOLATE CREPES

1   21-ounce box traditional fudge brownie mix
1   cup all-purpose flour
3   eggs, beaten
1½ cups milk
½   cup vegetable oil
1   cup butter
½   cup sugar
2   teaspoons vanilla
1   tablespoon lemon zest
6   large, firm ripe bananas, sliced
½   cup caramel ice cream topping
¾   cup whipped cream
2   tablespoons powdered sugar
¼   cup walnut gems

IN A LARGE BOWL, STIR TOGETHER BROWNIE MIX, flour, eggs, milk, and oil until smooth. Spray a 10-inch skillet with nonstick cooking spray; heat over medium heat. Pour about ¼ cup of the batter onto center of skillet. Immediately rotate skillet until a thin layer of batter covers bottom. Cook over medium heat about 1 minute, turning once, until top appears slightly dry. Remove crepe to cutting board, flipping crepe over so first cooked side is facing up. Immediately roll up crepe and place on plate to cool. Cover with kitchen towel. Repeat with remaining batter. In a large saucepan, cook butter and sugar over medium heat, stirring frequently, until sugar is dissolved. Remove from heat. Stir in vanilla and lemon zest until well mixed. Add banana slices; gently toss until coated and slightly softened.

For your picky eaters, serve crepes unfilled. For everyone else, fill 1 crepe at a time, keeping remaining crepes covered. Gently unroll crepe and fill with slightly less than ¼ cup banana filling. Reroll your crepe; place seam-side down on platter. Repeat with remaining crepes. Top crepes with drizzled caramel and a dollop of whipped topping. Sprinkle some powdered sugar and walnut gems on top. What a breakfast!

Serves 6 to 8.

WEEK 13

This week's meal is fairly simple and very versatile. You can follow the strudel recipe as written or create your own filling, such as broccoli with cheddar cheese. You could also make modifications to the recipe below, such as omitting the mushrooms and green onions if your kids are of the super-picky variety. The sauce can be used as a dipping sauce or to cover the strudels—it's really all up to you. I like to serve the strudel with the pretzel salad recipe included here, as well as sliced watermelon in the summer months or with sliced bananas, oranges, and apples in the winter months.

HAM AND CHEESE STRUDEL SOAKED IN SAUCE

2   cups diced honey ham
1   cup shredded Swiss cheese
1   cup diced mushrooms
¼   cup chopped green onions
1   egg, beaten
1   package Azumaya® Rectangular Wraps
½   cup butter, melted
½   cup sour cream
½   cup mayonnaise or salad dressing
2   tablespoons dry mustard, or 4 tablespoons Dijon mustard
1   teaspoon sugar

PREHEAT OVEN TO 350 DEGREES. In medium bowl combine ham, cheese, mushrooms, green onion, and egg. Mix well. Place a rectangluar wrap on a plate. Brush lightly with melted butter. Place 2 tablespoons of ham mixture in center of the dough square. Fold edges over ham mixture and then roll like a burrito. Place strudel, seam-side down, on ungreased baking sheet. Bake for 10 minutes.

In a small saucepan, combine sour cream, mayonnaise or salad dressing, dry mustard or Dijon mustard, and sugar. Cook and stir over low heat until warm. Pour sauce over ham strudels or pass it for dipping.

Serves 8.

Raspberry Pretzel Salad

2⅔   cups crushed pretzels
1   cup butter, melted
12   ounces cream cheese, softened
1½   cups sugar
2   8-ounce tubs thawed Cool Whip®, divided
1   6-ounce package raspberry gelatin
2   cups pineapple juice or water
1   16-ounce package frozen raspberries

PREHEAT OVEN TO 400 DEGREES. Place crushed pretzels and butter in bottom of a 9x13-inch baking dish; mix well and spread evenly in pan. Bake 10 minutes. While pretzel mixture is baking, mix cream cheese and sugar with an electric mixer until smooth. Spread cream cheese mixture over top of warm—not hot—baked pretzels. Do this very carefully so you don't lift the crust while spreading. Spread 1 tub of Cool Whip on top of cream cheese layer. Chill. Dissolve gelatin in boiling pineapple juice or water. Remove from heat and stir in raspberries. Refrigerate for 2 hours to allow gelatin to thicken almost to jelled point. Pour thickened gelatin over cream cheese layer. Spread the second tub of Cool Whip over mixture and refrigerate for 2 more hours.

Serves 8 to 10.

Week 14

This week's recipes are all about having fun. If your kids seem hesitant to try any of the dishes, tell them the names of the recipes. Many kids can't resist eating a "little pig" or a dish of dirt. The main recipe is extremely versatile. You can add diced carrots, green beans, or fresh bell peppers. It tastes great served with fresh cantaloupe and raspberries. Fresh cut avocados with a squeeze of lime juice and salt and pepper are also great accompaniments.

Little Pig in the Rice

1   cup brown rice
1   pound mild Italian turkey sausage or pork sausage
1   cup chopped onion
1   15-ounce can black beans, rinsed and drained
1   14.5-ounce can diced tomatoes, undrained
1   15.25-ounce can whole kernel corn with red and green bell peppers, drained
1   cup shredded Monterey Jack cheese

PREPARE RICE ACCORDING TO PACKAGE DIRECTIONS. While rice is cooking, brown sausage in a large nonstick skillet over medium-high heat until no pink remains, stirring frequently to break up sausage. Remove sausage from skillet; cover with foil to keep warm. Drain excess fat from skillet. In same skillet cook onion for 2 minutes. Add beans, undrained tomatoes, corn, sausage, and cooked rice. Heat through. Sprinkle cheese on top and serve.

Serves 6 to 8.

CREAMY CHEDDAR SALAD

2   16-ounce packages frozen peas, thawed
½   cup diced cheddar cheese
½   cup diced mozzarella cheese
1   medium onion, chopped
1   cup mayonnaise or salad dressing
    Salt and pepper, to taste
4   strips bacon, cooked crisp and crumbled

IN A LARGE BOWL, COMBINE PEAS, CHEESES, onions, mayonnaise, and salt and pepper to taste. Mix well. Chill until served. Just before serving, sprinkle crumbled bacon on top.

P.S. Tell the children they can have dirt for dessert if they eat their peas.
  Serves 4 to 6.

DISH OF DIRT

22   Oreo® Cookies, finely crushed (about 2 cups), divided
1   pint chocolate ice cream
    Chocolate flavored syrup
    Gummy worms, for garnish
    Whipped cream, for garnish

IN EACH OF 4 DESSERT DISHES, PLACE 2 tablespoons cookie crumbs. Top each with ½ cup ice cream, remaining 2 tablespoons cookie crumbs, and 1 tablespoon chocolate syrup. Garnish with gummy worms and whipped cream.

  Serves 4.

WEEK 15

Flowers are beautiful—especially on dark, stormy days. Let your children help you make these delicious recipes. They are easy and so very tasty!

EVERYDAY WREATH

2   18-ounce tubes refrigerated crescent roll dough
1   8-ounce package cream cheese, softened*
½   cup Miracle Whip®
½   pound cubed ham
2   cups grated cheese (Asiago or Havarti cheese are both great, but kids might prefer plain old cheddar)

PREHEAT OVEN TO 350 DEGREES. Spread croissant roll dough into a sunflower shape, with the thicker part of the croissant dough turned toward the center and the top of the triangle facing out, on a baking stone or a cookie sheet; set aside. In a large bowl, combine remaining ingredients. Spread on widest part of the sunflower shape. Roll the dough towards the inside, making it look like a wreath. Tuck the dough edges under and press so it is tight. Bake for 20 minutes, until golden brown on top.

Serves 4 to 6.

Mix into the cream cheese any other ingredients that you know are your children's favorites, for example, other meats or cheeses, broccoli, carrots, or fresh, chopped tomatoes.

ORANGE FLUFF

2   8-ounce packages instant tapioca pudding
1   3-ounce package orange gelatin
1½ cups boiling water
2   8-ounce tubs Cool Whip®, thawed
2   11-ounce cans mandarin oranges, drained

COMBINE PUDDING AND GELATIN MIXES IN A medium saucepan. Pour in boiling water and stir, over medium-high heat, until gelatin is dissolved and mixture returns to a boil and thickens. Thick tapioca beads should be clear orange. Remove from heat and let sit until cool. Put cooled gelatin-pudding mixture in a large bowl, fold in Cool Whip and add the oranges. Chill until ready to serve.

Serves 4 to 6.

WEEK 16

Spring is the perfect time to cook up a light-tasting Italian pasta and treat your family to a delicious strawberry-shortcake dessert with a twist. Add some homemade breadsticks, and you're sure to please everyone at the table.

LEMON PARMESAN PASTA

1   pound dry fettuccini*
1   cup heavy cream
½   tablespoon butter
1   tablespoon lemon zest
    Juice of 1 lemon
1   cup grated Parmesan cheese
    Salt and pepper, to taste

PREPARE PASTA ACCORDING TO PACKAGE DIRECTIONS. While pasta is cooking, heat cream in a heavy saucepan over medium heat. Add butter and stir. Add lemon zest and juice. Bring to a boil. Reduce heat to low and stir in Parmesan cheese until melted. Add salt and pepper to taste. Drain pasta, place in a large serving bowl, and pour sauce over top. Stir well to coat noodles.

Serves 6.

Whole wheat or spinach fettuccini also works well in this recipe.

PIZZA DOUGH BREADSTICKS

1   tablespoon yeast
1½   cups lukewarm water
4   cups bread flour
2   tablespoons sugar
1   teaspoon salt
1   tablespoon wheat gluten (optional; it just makes it softer)

Cornmeal

⅓ cup butter, melted

Seasoned salt

PREHEAT OVEN TO 400 DEGREES. Dissolve yeast in warm water in a small bowl. Let stand 20 minutes; it will be frothy when ready. In a large bowl, combine flour, sugar, salt, and wheat gluten, if using. Stir in yeast and knead 5 minutes until dough is smooth and elastic. If using a bread mixer, knead for 10 minutes. Spray nonstick cooking spray inside a bowl. Place dough inside. Let dough rise 20 minutes to 1 hour until double in size. On a floured surface, roll dough 1-inch think into a 12x6-inch rectangle. Cut into 12 6-inch lengths. Sprinkle cornmeal on a cooking stone or cookie sheet and spread around until pan or stone is well coated. Roll each strand of dough in butter. With your fingers on each end, twist dough and lay on the pan or stone at least 2 inches apart. Sprinkle seasoned salt over the top and bake 10 to 12 minutes, until light brown.

Makes 12 breadsticks.

BANANA-SPLIT SHORTCAKE

Shortcake

2 cups all-purpose flour

½ cup sugar

1 tablespoon baking powder

¼ teaspoon salt

⅓ cup shortening

⅔ cup milk

1 egg, lightly beaten

Filling

1 cup sliced strawberries

1 tablespoon sugar

45

1   8-ounce can pineapple tidbits in juice, undrained
1   medium banana, sliced
½   cup chocolate flavored syrup
1   quart vanilla ice cream
¼   cup chopped almonds or any nut that you like
     Whipped cream

PREHEAT OVEN TO 375 DEGREES. Spray a cookie sheet with nonstick cooking spray.

For shortcakes, combine flour, the ½ cup sugar, baking powder, and salt in a medium sized bowl. Remove ¼ cup of the flour mixture and set aside. Using a butter knife or a pastry blender, cut in shortening until mixture resembles coarse crumbs the size of a pea. Add milk and beaten egg; stir just until dough clings together. Turn out onto sanitized kitchen counter top sprinkled with some of the reserved flour mixture. Knead gently 8 to 10 times, adding remaining reserved flour mixture as needed.

Roll dough to a ½-inch thickness with lightly floured rolling pin. Cut with round biscuit cutter or your favorite shape cookie cutter. Gather dough scraps and re-roll dough to make a total of 8 shortcake shapes.

Transfer shortcake shapes to prepared cookie sheet. Bake 17 to 19 minutes until golden brown. Remove shortcake shapes to a cooling rack and cool completely.

For the filling, gently toss strawberries with sugar in a small bowl; let stand for at least 30 minutes. Add pineapple, with juice, and banana to strawberries. Mix gently. Split shortcake shapes in half. For each serving, spoon 1 tablespoon chocolate syrup on serving plate; top with bottom half of shortcake. Scoop ice cream over bottom half. Spoon fruit mixture over ice cream. Top with nuts and whipped cream. Cover with top half of shortcake.

Serves 8.

WEEK 17

This week is picnic week, whether you spread your picnic quilt in the park or on the floor in your living room. The memories—and the food—will be worth the effort.

FINGER-LICKIN' GOOD

6   boneless, skinless chicken breasts
1   12-ounce bag plain, barbecue, or sour cream and onion potato chips
1   egg
2   tablespoons milk

PREHEAT OVEN TO 400 DEGREES. Cut the chicken into finger-sized pieces. Fill a large Ziploc bag with the potato chips. Seal the bag and crush the chips with the back of a wooden spoon.

In a small bowl, whisk the egg and milk together. Dip the chicken pieces into the egg and then add to the Ziploc bag and shake to coat. Remove chicken from the bag and place on an ungreased cookie sheet. Bake for 20 minutes, flipping halfway through the cooking time. Serve with barbecue sauce, salsa, or honey mustard.

Serves 6.

MACARONI SALAD

1   16-ounce package of small shell macaroni
½   cup cider vinegar
½   cup vegetable oil
     Dash salt
     Dash pepper
2   stalks celery, chopped

1   stalk green onion, chopped
½   cup chopped green or orange pepper
½   cup cucumber, chopped
1   4-ounce can deveined medium shrimp, rinsed
3   cups Miracle Whip®
1   teaspoon mustard
⅛   teaspoon salt
⅛   teaspoon ground black pepper
1   teaspoon vinegar
½   cup cream
3   tablespoons pickle juice
    Dried parsley, for garnish
    Seasoned salt, for garnish

Boil macaroni until it's not quite al dente; it should still be firm in the middle. Drain and rinse in cold water; set aside. In a small bowl, combine the cider vinegar, vegetable oil, dash of salt, and pepper. Pour over the macaroni and marinate in the refrigerator for several hours or overnight. Toss together the celery, onion, green pepper, cucumber, and shrimp. Add vegetable and shrimp mixture to the macaroni. Combine next seven ingredients in a small bowl and pour over the macaroni mixture. Sprinkle with dried parsley and seasoned salt. Serve.

Serves 6 to 8.

POTATO LOGS

6   russet potatoes
2   tablespoons salad oil
2   teaspoons seasoned salt
3   tablespoons parsley flakes
2   teaspoons garlic salt
½   cup grated Parmesan cheese

PREHEAT OVEN TO 350 DEGREES. Scrub, but don't peel, potatoes. Cut into thin wedges. Pour salad oil in 1 large Ziploc bag. In a second Ziploc bag, combine seasoned salt, parsley flakes, garlic salt, and Parmesan cheese. Put a handful of potatoes into the sack with oil and shake to coat lightly. Transfer potatoes to the spice mixture and shake well. Place on a cookie sheet that has been coated with nonstick cooking spray. If needed, re-supply dry ingredients and oil in Ziploc bags as needed to coat all the potatoes. Bake 45 minutes, until softened, browned, and crispy. Serve with sour cream or ketchup.

Serves 6.

WEEK 18

This week's recipes are some of my favorites. They are especially nice because you can make them ahead of time and freeze them. If you do so, freeze the puff pastries and gravy separately. Thaw dishes in the refrigerator overnight, pop pastries in the oven and warm the gravy on the stovetop. Serve with mashed potatoes and you have an instant meal! Good accompaniments for this dinner include carrot and celery sticks with ranch dressing for dipping or fresh, cut-up fruit.

CHICKEN PUFF PASTRIES

2   8-ounce cans chicken
½   cup butter, softened
1   8-ounce package cream cheese, softened
2   8-ounce cans Pillsbury® crescent rolls
2   .87-ounce packets chicken gravy mix
2   14-ounce cans chicken broth
1   teaspoon dried basil
1   teaspoon dried oregano
1   teaspoon poultry seasoning
1   teaspoon butter

PREHEAT OVEN TO 375 DEGREES. Mix chicken, softened butter, and cream cheese in a medium bowl. Open the cans of crescent rolls and lay out the dough. Put a tablespoon of filling inside each roll and form into crescent shapes. Bake on ungreased cookie sheet for 13 to 15 minutes.

To make gravy, whisk chicken gravy mix packets into broth in a medium saucepan. Make sure all lumps are gone. Add basil, oregano, poultry seasoning, and the 1 teaspoon butter. Whisk again. Heat over medium-high heat until gravy comes to a gentle, rolling boil. Stir occasionally to prevent gravy from burning. Reduce heat and let gravy simmer until the puff pastries are done. Serve pastries with gravy on top.

Serves 6 to 8.

TURTLE BARS

1   package refrigerated sugar cookie dough
2   cups semisweet chocolate chips, divided
3   cups pecans, chopped, divided
½   cup butter
½   cup brown sugar
1   jar caramel ice cream topping
1   cup graham cracker crumbs (about 16 squares)

PREHEAT OVEN TO 350 DEGREES. Press cookie dough evenly in the bottom of an ungreased 9x13-inch pan.

Sprinkle 1 cup of the chocolate chips and 1½ cups of the pecans over dough; lightly press into dough. Set aside.

In a medium-sized saucepan, melt butter over medium-high heat. Stir in brown sugar, caramel topping, and graham cracker crumbs. Heat to boiling, stirring constantly. Pour over dough in pan; spread evenly. Sprinkle with remaining chocolate chips and pecans.

Bake for 25 to 30 minutes, or until edges are a deep golden brown and pecans are lightly toasted. Cool on a cooling rack for 30 minutes. Loosen dough from the sides of the pan, but do not cut. Cool completely (about 3 hours). Cut into squares.

Makes 12 bars.

WEEK 19

Cinco de Mayo should be coming up soon by week 19 of the year. To celebrate the occasion, try out the fabulous quesadilla recipe below. You may also want to grab a few recipes from previous weeks, such as the Guacamole and Pico de Gallo to serve up with a big bowl of tortilla chips. Decorate the table with red, green, and white, and maybe even let the kids whack a piñata after dinner if they eat all their veggies. This meal is perfect for serving up with a large platter of cut vegetables and fresh fruit.

TEX-MEX QUESADILLAS WITH AVOCADO-TOMATO SALSA

2	teaspoons canola oil
1	green onion, thinly sliced
1	pound thinly sliced, boneless, skinless chicken breasts
1	teaspoon lime zest
1	teaspoon salt
1	teaspoon ground black pepper
2	tablespoons freshly squeezed lime juice
1	cup shredded Mexican cheese blend
4	12-inch burrito-size flour tortillas
½	avocado, diced
¾	cup salsa

IN A LARGE SKILLET, HEAT OIL OVER MEDIUM HEAT. Add green onion and cook about 6 minutes, or until tender, stirring occasionally. Cut chicken into 1-inch pieces and evenly sprinkle both sides of the chicken with lime zest, salt, and pepper. Add the chicken to green onion in the skillet; cook 10 minutes, or until chicken is no longer pink. Transfer to a bowl and stir in the lime juice. Evenly divide the chicken mixture and cheese between each of the four tortillas, placing mixture on only one half of each tortilla. Fold over tortillas to make 4 quesadillas.

In the same skillet, cook quesadillas on medium heat, browning the tortillas on both sides until heated throughout. Cut each quesadilla into thirds. Stir the chopped avocado into the salsa and serve alongside the quesadillas. Serves 4.

Frozen Delight

- 64 Nilla Wafers®, divided
- 1 cup flaked coconut, toasted
- ½ cup almonds, toasted, finely chopped
- ½ cup butter or margarine, melted
- 4 cups (1 quart) lime sherbet, softened
- 4 cups (1 quart) orange sherbet, softened
- 4 cups (1 quart) raspberry sherbet, softened

Preheat oven to 350 degrees. In a Ziploc bag, finely crush 37 of the 64 wafers with a rolling pin or cup. Mix wafer crumbs, coconut, almonds, and butter until well-blended. Press firmly into the bottom of a 9x13-inch baking dish or pan. Bake 8 to 10 minutes until lightly browned; cool. Spread a layer of lime sherbet over the cooled crust. Freeze until firm, then spread a layer of orange sherbet and a layer of raspberry sherbet, freezing between each layer. Freeze final dessert for at least 4 hours. Remove from freezer about 10 minutes prior to serving; let stand at room temperature to soften slightly. Cut into squares. Top each square with a wafer or two. Store any leftover dessert in the freezer.

Serves 12 to 24.

WEEK 20

Few things are as healthy as salmon. For that reason alone, it's well worth the effort to get your kids to eat it. This week's main dish is what finally convinced my kids that salmon is not only healthy but tastes good too. And have fun modifying the "Delightfully Green Salad" by substituting a new vegetable every time you make it.

SALMON FRY IN ASIAN NOODLES

1   teaspoon lemon zest
2   tablespoons freshly squeezed lemon juice
1   teaspoon lime zest
2   tablespoons freshly squeezed lime juice
6   6-ounce salmon fillets
    Salt and pepper, to taste
2   6.75-ounce packages rice noodles, stir-fry or linguine style
2   tablespoons Asian fish sauce
½   cup pecan gems or almonds (optional)
2   green onions, thinly sliced (optional)

PREHEAT OVEN TO 400 DEGREES. Coat a 9x13-inch glass baking dish with nonstick cooking spray. Grate your zests and squeeze your juices and set aside for easy access during preparation.

Arrange salmon in prepared baking dish and sprinkle with lemon and lime zests and salt and pepper to taste. Roast 10 to 12 minutes or until just opaque in color throughout. Meanwhile, prepare rice noodles according to package directions, reserving ¼ cup of the cooking water before draining noodles. In a medium bowl combine lemon juice, lime juice, fish sauce, and nuts, if using. Stir in noodles and reserved cooking water; toss to combine. Serve the salmon fillets over noodles; if desired, sprinkle with sliced green onions to garnish.

Serves 6.

DELIGHTFULLY GREEN SALAD

1   bag spring salad mix, washed
1   bag spinach, washed
1   tomato, chopped
1   head broccoli, washed and chopped
½   jicama, peeled and sliced into strips
1   cup sprouts, your choice (I like alfalfa)
½   cup fresh or frozen peas, thawed if frozen
½   cup canned beets
½   cup chopped celery
½   cup sesame seeds
1   recipe Buttermilk Ranch Dressing (see recipe below)

TOSS ALL INGREDIENTS, EXCEPT THE DRESSING, in a large salad bowl. Chill until ready to serve. Dress with Buttermilk Ranch Dressing when serving.
Serves 6 to 8.

BUTTERMILK RANCH DRESSING

½   cup buttermilk
½   cup low-fat mayonnaise
2   tablespoons chopped fresh parsley leaves
2   tablespoons chopped fresh chives
1   tablespoon apple cider vinegar
1   teaspoon minced garlic
½   teaspoon salt
½   teaspoon ground black pepper

WHISK TOGETHER ALL INGREDIENTS IN A MEDIUM BOWL. Serve immediately or chill in the refrigerator up to 5 days.
Makes 1½ cups.

WEEK 21

Every Friday night is a pizza and movie night for our family. We love being together and making our own pizzas. It's fun to watch the children get creative. My son and daughter once actually built a 3-D pizza and made a ship with masts and sails. It didn't survive the storm in the oven, but it was so much fun. Include a fresh salad and your kids' favorite dressing to accompany your pizza fest.

IT'S PIZZA NIGHT

1   3-pound bag Rhodes® Frozen Dinner Rolls
     Cornmeal
1   10-ounce bottle Ragu® Pizza Sauce
     Toppings of your choice, which might include:
     Shredded mozzarella cheese
     Shredded cheddar cheese
     Canadian bacon
     Pineapple chunks
     Pepperoni slices
     Chopped olives
     Sliced mushrooms
     Cooked Italian sausage

PREHEAT OVEN TO 350 DEGREES. Place 12 frozen balls of dough on a plate and microwave for 2 minutes on high power. The dough should be pliable but still cold. Smash the dough flat on a plate and then let the children stretch each piece out into a wide circle or whatever shapes they like.

Set out all the toppings so the children can put the sauce on, then the cheese, then whatever else they want. Place ½ cup of cornmeal on a baking stone or cookie sheet. Spread to cover pan. Place pizzas atop the cornmeal on the stone or the cookie sheet. Bake for 20 minutes, or until dough is lightly browned on edges. Serve, then start all over again until everyone is full.

Serves 24.

Peanut Butter Yummies

- 1   cup sugar
- 1   cup light corn syrup
- 1   cup peanut butter
- 2½ cups Rice Chex® cereal
- 2½ cups Rice Krispies® cereal

Combine the sugar and corn syrup in a medium saucepan. Bring to a boil over medium-high heat, stirring often. Maintain a rolling boil for about 1 minute. Remove from heat. Add the peanut butter to the hot syrup and stir until thoroughly mixed. Combine cereals in a large bowl. Pour hot peanut butter syrup over the cereals and stir with a large wooden spoon. Spoon cookie-sized amounts onto waxed paper and let cool before serving.

Makes 2 dozen.

WEEK 22

This week, try a fun recipe for children that will lighten things up and bring an array of laughter and fun to your dinner table. It may also open the way for other positive and creative events to occur around the table. After all, who wouldn't be interested in a conversation about the octopus you're eating for dinner? If your kids don't like Alfredo sauce, try mixing the shells and vegetables in a little olive oil instead, or simply use jarred tomato sauce or even a package of shells and cheese. I like to serve kid-friendly fruit, such as banana slices and mandarin oranges, with the Octopus and Shells.

OCTOPUS AND SHELLS

6   hot dogs
3   cups uncooked small shell pasta
2   cups frozen mixed vegetables
1   15-ounce jar Alfredo sauce
    Yellow mustard in a squeeze bottle
    Cheese-flavored fish-shaped crackers

YOU ARE GOING TO CREATE AN OCTOPUS. To do so, place 1 hot dog on its side with one end facing you. Slice hot dog in half vertically, beginning 1 inch from the end nearest you. Roll the hot dog a quarter turn and slice in half vertically again, making 4 segments that are connected at the top. Slice each segment in half vertically, creating a total of 8 legs. Repeat with the remaining hot dogs.

Place hot dogs in medium saucepan; cover with water. Bring to a boil over high heat. Remove from heat and set aside. Prepare the pasta according to the package directions, stirring vegetables into the water during the last few minutes of cooking time. Drain and return to pan. Stir in the Alfredo sauce. Warm mixture over low heat until heated through. Divide pasta mixture between 6 plates. Drain your octopus-dogs. Arrange one octopus on top of pasta mixture on each plate. Draw faces on the "heads" of the octo-dogs with mustard. Sprinkle fish crackers over the pasta mixture.

Serves 6.

BROWNIE SANDWICH COOKIES

1   21-ounce package Duncan Hines® Chocolate Lovers Double
    Fudge Brownie Mix
1   egg
3   tablespoons water
    Sugar
1   16-ounce tub cream cheese frosting
    Red food coloring (optional)
½   cup semisweet mini chocolate chips

PREHEAT OVEN TO 375 DEGREES. Grease 2 cookie sheets. In a large bowl, combine brownie mix, fudge packet from mix, egg, and water. Stir until well blended. Shape dough into 50 1-inch balls. Place balls 2 inches apart on prepared cookie sheets. Grease bottom of a drinking glass, then dip in sugar. Press each cookie gently to flatten it to a 3/8 inch thickness. Dip glass in sugar each time and repeat the process. Bake for 6 to 7 minutes, or until set. Cool 1 minute on cookie sheets. Remove to cooling racks and cool completely.

For the filling, tint frosting with red food coloring, if desired. Stir in chocolate chips. To assemble, spread 1 tablespoon frosting on bottom of one cookie and top with the second cookie. Press together to make a great sandwich. Repeat with remaining cookies.

Makes about 25 sandwich cookies.

WEEK 23

Never heard of Captain Crunch cereal for dinner? Well, now you have. The secret in this week's main recipe is the Captain Crunch. Just knowing that a yummy breakfast cereal is part of dinner will make kids eager to dig in. This is a great main course or a wonderful appetizer.

CHICKEN CRUNCH

3	cups Captain Crunch® cereal
1	cup Cornflakes® cereal
½	teaspoon onion powder
½	teaspoon garlic powder
½	teaspoon salt
½	teaspoon pepper
1	egg
1	cup milk
4	boneless, skinless chicken breast halves cut into bite-sized pieces*

PREHEAT OVEN TO 375 DEGREES. Put the cereals in a Ziploc bag and crush with a rolling pin or a cup. Combine crushed cereals, onion powder, garlic powder, salt, and pepper in a medium bowl. In another medium mixing bowl, beat the egg with a fork. Stir in the milk. Dredge chicken in the milk and egg mixture. With a slotted spoon, remove the chicken from the egg mixture, and then toss it in the dry mixture until the chicken is evenly coated. Place chicken pieces on a cookie sheet coated with nonstick cooking spray and bake for 20 minutes, until golden brown. Serve with Tangy Mustard Sauce (recipe following) or your favorite barbecue sauce.

Serves 4 to 6.

Chicken that is slightly frozen is much easier to cut into pieces—and saves a lot of prep time.

TANGY MUSTARD SAUCE

2   tablespoons Grey Poupon® Country Dijon Mustard
3   tablespoons mayonnaise
1   teaspoon yellow mustard
1   teaspoon creamy style horseradish sauce
1   teaspoon honey

COMBINE ALL INGREDIENTS IN A SMALL BOWL. Chill until ready to serve. If you are a "saucy" person, you had better double or triple this recipe, because it is good. You can also serve this on grilled chicken or atop a green salad.
    Serves 4 to 6.

QUICK SUMMER SLAW

1   16-ounce package coleslaw
1   bunch green onions, finely chopped
½   cup shelled sunflower seeds
½   cup slivered or sliced almonds
½   cup olive oil
3   tablespoons sugar
3   tablespoons apple cider, balsamic, or raspberry vinegar (your choice)
1   package chicken-flavored ramen noodles

TOSS COLESLAW, GREEN ONIONS, SUNFLOWER SEEDS, and almonds together in a large bowl. In a smaller bowl, whisk together oil, sugar, vinegar, and the seasoning packet from the noodles until well blended. Just before serving, stir in dry, crushed ramen noodles.
    Serves 4 to 6.

PEAR ICE

1 28-ounce can pears, chilled
4 cups ice

POUR CHILLED PEARS, INCLUDING JUICE, into blender. Add the ice and blend. Serve in dessert glasses or freeze into popsicles.

Serves 4 to 6.

WEEK 24

This is one of those take-it-out-of-the-can recipes and cooks perfectly every time. And the flavors balance nicely with the wonderful fruit salad and dressing.

SMOTHERED BURRITOS

10 12-inch burrito-size flour tortillas
1   15-ounce can refried beans
4   cups shredded cheddar cheese
1   cup sour cream
1   10-ounce can mild enchilada sauce
1   cup chopped, fresh cilantro leaves

PREHEAT OVEN TO 350 DEGREES. Spray a 9x13 baking dish with nonstick cooking spray. Place a tortilla on a plate and fill with 1 tablespoon of refried beans, 1 tablespoon of cheese, and 1 teaspoon of sour cream. Fold sides of tortilla to the middle and roll burrito closed. Set burrito in baking dish. Repeat until all the tortillas have been filled, rolled, and set in the dish. Pour enchilada sauce evenly over burritos. Top with the remaining cheese and cilantro. Cover with aluminum foil and bake for 30 minutes.

Serves 6 to 8.

MEXICAN FRUIT SALAD

3   red apples, unpeeled, cored, and cut into wedges
¼   cup fresh lemon or lime juice, divided
2   avocados
3   oranges, peeled and sliced crosswise
1   pineapple, peeled, cored, and cubed
1   pint strawberries, cleaned and halved

1   bunch red leaf lettuce, washed and shredded
¾   cup flaked coconut
2   tablespoons sunflower seeds
1   recipe Lime Dressing (see recipe below)

TOSS APPLE WEDGES IN 2 TABLESPOONS OF THE lemon or lime juice and set aside. Peel avocados and cut into wedges, toss in remaining lemon or lime juice. Group apples, avocados, orange slices, pineapple, and strawberries on a bed of lettuce. Sprinkle coconut and sunflower seeds over fruit. Serve with Lime Dressing drizzled on top; or, if desired, allow children to dish up fruit and top with coconut, sunflower seeds, and dressing, if desired.

Serves 6 to 8.

LIME DRESSING

1   cup sugar
¼   cup water
1   teaspoon lime zest
    Juice of 2 limes

COMBINE SUGAR AND WATER IN SMALL SAUCEPAN; bring to a boil over medium-high heat, stirring occasionally. Remove from heat; stir in lime zest and juice. Cool and refrigerate several hours before serving.

Makes 1½ cups.

WEEK 25

Why open a bag of frozen fish sticks, when you can create your own, authentic fish and chips? Kids will be fascinated with how quickly the fish cooks up in hot oil and how crisp and brown the runny batter turns. Serve with a great salad, such as the coleslaw recipe included here, and finish off with a chocolaty dessert. This is the perfect way to end your week!

FISHING FOR CHIPS

1	pound frozen or fresh fish fillets, such as tilapia, cod, or halibut
1	pound baking potatoes, peeled
½	cup all-purpose flour, divided
1	teaspoon salt
2	tablespoons water
1	tablespoon cooking oil, plus additional oil for frying
1	egg yolk
1	egg white, stiffly beaten
	Salt
	Malt vinegar

IF FROZEN, THAW FISH. CUT FISH INTO serving-size pieces. Pat dry with a paper towel; set aside.

Cut potatoes into uniform strips slightly larger than French fries. Heat oil in a large pot. Add potatoes, a few at a time, and fry until golden brown, 5 to 6 minutes. Remove with a slotted spoon, drain, and keep warm. Make sure oil stays hot enough to fry as you prepare the batter for the fish.

In a shallow bowl, stir together ¼ cup of the flour and 1 teaspoon salt. Make a well in the center of the dry ingredients. Pour water, 1 tablespoon oil, and egg yolk into the hole; beat until smooth. Fold in egg white. Put remaining ¼ cup flour in another shallow dish. Dredge fish pieces in the flour and then in the batter. Fry fish in deep hot oil until golden brown, about 1 to 2 minutes on each side. Do this in batches, as crowding the pan will lower the temperature of the oil. Drain fish on paper towels. To serve, season fish and chips with salt and drizzle with malt vinegar.

Serves 4.

TARTAR SAUCE

2	tablespoons dill pickle relish
1	cup mayonnaise
1	teaspoon lemon juice
½	teaspoon dill weed

WHISK RELISH AND MAYONNAISE TOGETHER in a small bowl. Add lemon juice and dill weed. Stir well. Chill until ready to serve.

Makes 1 cup.

KENTUCKY STYLE COLESLAW

8	cups finely shredded cabbage
¼	cup diced or shredded carrots
2	tablespoons minced onions
⅓	cup sugar
½	teaspoon salt
⅛	teaspoon pepper
¼	cup milk
½	cup mayonnaise
¼	cup buttermilk
1½	tablespoons vinegar
1	tablespoon lemon juice

COMBINE ALL INGREDIENTS IN A LARGE BOWL and chill for at least 2 hours before serving.

Serves 6 to 8.

CHOCOLATE CREAM CRUNCH

1   cup all-purpose flour
1   cup finely chopped pecans
½   cup margarine, softened
1   8-ounce package cream cheese, softened
1   cup powdered sugar
1   8-ounce tub Cool Whip®, thawed and divided
1   6-ounce package instant chocolate pudding
1   6-ounce package instant vanilla pudding
3   cups milk, divided

PREHEAT OVEN TO 350 DEGREES. Make crust by combining flour, pecans, and margarine in a small bowl. Press into bottom of 9x13-inch pan. Bake 20 minutes. Cool completely on wire rack.

Blend cream cheese and powdered sugar with an electric mixer until fluffy. Fold in 1 cup of the Cool Whip. Blend well and spread over cooled crust. Chill. Combine instant chocolate pudding and 1½ cups milk. Mix until smooth. Pour over cream cheese layer. Chill. Pudding will thicken in refrigerator. Repeat with instant vanilla pudding. Chill. Frost with remaining Cool Whip. Cut into 4-inch squares and serve.

Makes 28 squares.

WEEK 26

Nothing soothes the soul more than a real tasty bowl of soup—and this week's comfort foods will make everyone happy and satisfied.

CHICKEN TORTILLA SOUP

2	tablespoons olive oil
2	boneless skinless chicken breasts, cut into bite-sized pieces
1	onion, chopped
2	teaspoons minced garlic
1	4.5-ounce can green chilies, chopped
1	14.5-ounce can crushed tomatoes
2	14-ounce cans chicken broth
1	10-ounce can enchilada sauce
1	10-ounce package frozen corn
2	15-ounce cans black beans, drained and rinsed
1	15-ounce can tomato sauce
1	teaspoon chili powder
1	teaspoon ground cumin
1	tablespoon seasoned salt
¼	cup red wine vinegar
2	teaspoons lime juice
¼	cup fresh, chopped cilantro leaves
	Sour cream, for garnish
	Shredded cheddar cheese, for garnish
	Tortilla chips

HEAT OLIVE OIL IN A LARGE SKILLET OVER MEDIUM HEAT. Sauté chicken pieces, onion, and garlic until chicken is white. Add remaining ingredients, with the exception of the sour cream, cheese, and chips. Bring to a rolling boil and then reduce heat and simmer for 15 to 20 minutes. Ladle into bowls and top each with a dollop of sour cream, a sprinkling of cheese, and tortilla chips.

Serves 6 to 8.

MEXICAN SOPAS

- 15   Rhodes® Frozen Dinner Rolls
       Canola oil
- 5   tablespoons ground cinnamon
- 1   cup sugar
- 1   cup honey
- 1   cup butter

PUT RHODES ROLLS ON A PLATE AND MICROWAVE on high power for about 2 minutes. Rolls should be pliable but cool. Stretch and pull dough to desired size of scone. Heat 2 to 3 inches oil in a large pot. Add scones to the oil, a few at a time, and cook about 1 minute on each side, until golden brown. Drain on paper towels.

In a separate bowl, mix cinnamon and sugar. Take warm, finished scones and roll them in sugar mixture. If you prefer honey butter, beat the honey and softened butter until smooth and creamy. Serve with scones.

Makes 15 scones.

WEEK 27

This week's recipes are new versions of classic recipes that taste great every time. Decorate the table with a Western theme and have the family come to dinner in cowboy boots and blue jeans. You can even play your favorite country-western music during dinner. Yee-ha!

CATTLEMAN'S EASY CATCH

1	3- to 4-pound boneless beef chuck roast
½	cup chopped onion
1	teaspoon salt
1	teaspoon garlic powder
1	teaspoon ground black pepper
¼	teaspoon ground cloves
2	bay leaves
2	14-ounce cans beef broth
½	cup cider vinegar
8 to 12	hamburger buns, split
	Lettuce leaves
	Barbecue sauce
	Horseradish sauce, if desired

TRIM FAT FROM MEAT. Place meat in a 4-quart or larger slow cooker, cutting meat to fit. Add onion, salt, garlic powder, pepper, cloves, bay leaves, and beef broth. Pour vinegar over all. Cover and cook on low heat overnight for 8 to 10 hours until meat is very tender. Remove meat from slow cooker. Using 2 forks, shred meat. Serve in buns with lettuce leaves, barbecue sauce, and creamy horseradish sauce, if desired.

Serves 8 to 12.

Everyone's Favorite Potato Salad

4	russet potatoes
4	tablespoons dill pickle juice
3	tablespoons finely chopped dill pickles
¼	cup chopped, fresh Italian parsley
½	cup chopped red onion
2	stalks celery, chopped
1	scallion, chopped
2	hard-boiled eggs, chopped
⅔	cup mayonnaise
2	teaspoons Dijon mustard
	Salt and pepper, to taste

Bring a large pot of water to a boil over high heat. Add the potatoes with the skins on. Boil for 20 minutes. Take out potatoes and let cool enough to handle. Peel off skins. Dice potatoes into bite-sized squares and transfer to a large bowl. Add the pickle juice, pickles, parsley, red onion, celery, scallion, and boiled eggs. In a separate bowl, mix mayonnaise, Dijon mustard, salt, and pepper. Add to the potatoes. Mix well. Chill for at least 2 hours before serving. This will give all the spices and tastes a chance to blend together.

Serves 6 to 8.

WEEK 28

Spice things up a little this week. Let the kids help you assemble the enchiladas and teach them about some of the ingredients in this week's dish. This will encourage them to try what they've made. A simple search on the Internet will teach you about the ingredients so you can teach your children and enjoy an afternoon of cooking together.

BEEF ENCHILADAS

3 pounds sirloin steak or beef roast

1 14-ounce can beef broth

2 teaspoons chili powder

1 teaspoon minced garlic

2 teaspoons cumin

1 teaspoon dried basil

1 teaspoon dried oregano

1 cup chopped onion

2 teaspoons seasoned salt

1 12-ounce package corn tortillas

½ cup fresh salsa

2 cups shredded cheddar cheese, divided

2 7.5-ounce cans diced green chilies

¾ cup chopped black olives

1 10-ounce can enchilada sauce

½ cup chopped, fresh cilantro leaves

½ cup sour cream

THE MORNING OF, PLACE STEAK OR BEEF ROAST in a slow cooker. Pour broth over the top. Sprinkle with chili powder, garlic, cumin, basil, oregano, onion, and seasoned salt. Simmer on low for 8 hours. When done, shred meat with 2 forks.

When ready to prepare enchiladas, preheat oven to 350 degrees. Coat casserole dish with nonstick cooking spray.

Spoon a little of the meat mixture into the center of each corn tortilla. Add small amounts of salsa, cheddar cheese—reserving ½ cup for later— green chilies, and olives. Fold tortillas up and place in the casserole dish.

Pour enchilada sauce over tortillas. Top with remaining ½ cup shredded cheese and cilantro. Cover with aluminum foil. Bake 30 minutes in the preheated oven. Garnish with a dollop of sour cream.

Serves 6 to 8.

Leftover meat can be refrigerated for 3 to 5 days or frozen for up to 6 months.

MANGO MASH-UP

    3   mangoes, peeled and sliced
    1   tray ice cubes
    2   tablespoons lime juice
    1   cup sugar
    1   teaspoon vanilla
    ¾   cup frozen orange juice concentrate
    1   2-liter bottle of ginger ale

COMBINE MANGOES, ICE, LIME JUICE, SUGAR, vanilla, and orange juice concentrate in the jar of a blender. Pulse until well blended. Add ginger ale until blender jar is nearly full. Blend again and enjoy.

Serves 4.

WEEK 29

This week, spice things up with some friendly competitions. Play some mariachi music and have a dance-off. Or see who can build the biggest tower of Oreos. The best part? Everyone wins with these delicious recipes!

TACO SALAD

1   pound meat (boneless chicken, ground chuck, or vegetarian ground meat crumbles)
1   tablespoon minced garlic
1   teaspoon salt
1   teaspoon ground black pepper
1   teaspoon chili powder
1   teaspoon garlic powder
1   teaspoon cumin
1   head romaine lettuce, chopped
3   large tomatoes, diced
1   medium sweet yellow onion or 1 red onion, chopped
1   cup buttermilk
1   6-ounce packet Hidden Valley Ranch® Buttermilk Dressing
1   cup mayonnaise
1   bag tortilla chips
2   cups shredded Colby Jack or cheddar cheese

COOK MEAT IN A LARGE SKILLET OVER MEDIUM-HIGH HEAT. As meat cooks, add minced garlic, salt, pepper, chili powder, garlic powder, and cumin to skillet. Work seasonings into the meat and cook until meat is cooked through; set aside. Prepare bowls with chopped lettuce, tomatoes, and onion. In a medium-sized bowl, mix buttermilk, Hidden Valley Ranch packet, and mayonnaise. Whisk until mixed well. To serve taco salads, instruct family members to layer their plates with tortilla chips, then lettuce, meat, vegetables, dressing, and cheese. Encourage kids to try as many ingredients as they can; but remember that sometimes it's best to start out small. Be enthusiastic if they use even just a few toppings.

Serves 6 to 8.

BAJA BEANS

3	15-ounce cans black or pinto beans, drained and rinsed
½	cup butter
1	handful chopped, fresh cilantro leaves
1	tablespoon chopped garlic
1	teaspoon chili powder
1	tablespoon ground cumin
2	teaspoons seasoned salt
1	teaspoon dried oregano

COMBINE ALL INGREDIENTS IN A LARGE POT. Bring to a boil, stirring often, then simmer for 30 minutes. (Or make the night before and reheat.) Great as a side dish or in enchiladas, tacos, or burritos.

Serves 6 to 8.

LEANING TOWER OF OREOS

4	cups (1 quart) chocolate fudge swirl ice cream
	Oreos®
	Mint fudge sauce
	Whipped cream

BUILD A TOWER OF OREOS BY ALTERNATING A COOKIE with a spoonful of ice cream. Drizzle fudge sauce over the top and finish with a crown of whipped cream.

Serves 6.

WEEK 30

Have a sweet and sour night this week. As your kids eat the meal, have them talk about things that make them feel sweet/good and things that make them feel sour/bad. It will be a great conversation starter. You could also promise them a bag of sweet and sour treats (just buy a variety of candy) for dessert if they eat all of the veggies. Or, have something sweet, like sherbet, and something sour, like lemon drops, for dessert. If you want to save time this week, buy a bag of frozen stir-fry pepper strips at the store instead of using fresh peppers.

SWEET AND SOUR CHICKEN

2	tablespoons olive oil
1	pound chicken breasts, semi-frozen and cut into cubes
½	teaspoon salt
4	tablespoons soy sauce, divided
⅓	cup sugar
1	14-ounce can chicken broth
4	tablespoons cornstarch
4	tablespoons red wine vinegar or cider vinegar
⅓	cup pineapple juice
½	cup ketchup
⅔	cup pineapple tidbits
½	cup grated carrots
4 to 6	cups cooked rice

HEAT OIL IN A LARGE SKILLET OVER MEDIUM HEAT. Add chicken cubes, salt, and 2 tablespoons of the soy sauce. Sauté until chicken is tender and browned.

In a large saucepan blend sugar, chicken broth, cornstarch, vinegar, pineapple juice, ketchup, and remaining soy sauce until smooth. Slowly stir in meat, including the juices that form at the bottom of the skillet. Add pineapple tidbits and grated carrot. Stir and simmer for 5 minutes.

Serve over hot rice.

Serves 6.

TRADITIONAL FRIED RICE

1   green onion, chopped
2   eggs
1   teaspoon salt
    Pepper to taste
4   tablespoons oil, divided
4   cups cold cooked rice
½   tablespoon light soy sauce, or oyster sauce, as desired

WASH AND FINELY CHOP GREEN ONION; set aside. In a small bowl, lightly beat eggs. Add salt and pepper. Heat a wok or frying pan and add 2 tablespoons oil. When the oil is hot, add eggs. Cook, stirring eggs until they are lightly scrambled. Remove eggs and clean out the pan. Add another 2 tablespoons oil. Add the cooked rice and stir-fry for 2 to 5 minutes, using a wooden spoon to stir the rice. Add soy sauce or oyster sauce, as desired. When the rice is heated through, add the scrambled eggs back into the pan.* Mix thoroughly. Stir in the green onion.

Serves 4.

*You can also add other ingredients like ham, pork, chicken, carrots, or peas to the rice at the same time you add the eggs.

WEEK 31

Treat your family to a gourmet meal this week. Use your best tablecloth, as well as matching china and goblets. Use the occasion to teach children a lesson in manners. Let the boys hold the chairs for the girls. Encourage kids to say please and thank you often and to wait until everyone is served before eating. It will be a wonderful memory, and the effects of the lesson will carry on for years.

PORK CHOPS IN GINGER CREAM SAUCE

6 to 8   boneless pork chops, about 1-inch thick

Overnight marinade

2   12-ounce cans Coca-Cola®

Second marinade

1   cup pineapple juice

¼   cup lemon juice

½   cup soy sauce

1   cup frozen orange juice concentrate

¾   cup freshly grated gingerroot, divided

2   tablespoons seasoned salt

2   teaspoons chopped garlic

Sauce

2   tablespoons olive oil

4   cups heavy cream
    Freshly chopped Italian parsley, for garnish
    Paprika, for garnish

THE NIGHT BEFORE SERVING, PLACE PORK CHOPS in a large bowl and pour Coca-Cola on top and cover with plastic wrap. Refrigerate overnight to marinate. The next day, discard cola marinade and pour in pineapple juice, lemon juice, soy sauce, orange juice concentrate, ½ cup of the grated ginger, seasoned salt, and garlic. Stir until well mixed. Let marinate at least 4 hours in the refrigerator. When ready to prepare, discard marinade. Heat a large skillet over medium heat. Using 2 tablespoons olive oil, brown chops on both sides. To prevent overcooking the chops, cook about 2 minutes per side. Be sure to cut into the meat to make sure it is not pink in the center.

While chops cook, pour cream and remaining grated ginger in a large skillet and whisk gently over low heat until thoroughly warmed. The cream will take on the gentle taste of ginger. When meat is finished, ladle ½ cup of the ginger cream sauce on each plate. Place a chop on top of the sauce and spoon a serving of Coconut Jasmine Rice on one side and Steamed Lemon Asparagus on the other. Sprinkle with fresh parsley and a little bit of paprika. Not only is this a beautiful dish, but it is so tasty.

Serves 6 to 8.

COCONUT JASMINE RICE

    4   cups uncooked jasmine rice
    2   14-ounce cans coconut milk
    2   tablespoons lime juice
         Dash nutmeg

FOLLOW PACKAGE DIRECTIONS FOR COOKING THE RICE, substituting 4 of the cups of water with the coconut milk and including lime juice and nutmeg. Serve hot. You can cook this in a rice cooker as well. Just add everything and set the cooker to steam on brown rice setting. Jasmine rice is a rice from Thailand. It has a fragrant nutty flavor that you won't soon forget.

Serves 6 to 8.

STEAMED LEMON VEGETABLES

2 quarts water
1 pound of your favorite vegetable (carrots, asparagus, broccoli)
2 tablespoons lemon zest
1 teaspoon seasoned salt

IN A LARGE POT, BRING 2 QUARTS WATER to a rapid boil. Place vegetables into the pot. Blanch for 1 minute. Using tongs, fish out vegetables and put in a glass dish. Sprinkle lemon zest and seasoned salt on top. Cover with aluminum foil and keep in warm oven until ready to serve.

Serves 6.

WEEK 32

Make this week all about color and texture by trying this Asian-themed meal. Kids can help fill the wontons and will gobble up the crispy wonton chips. If the flavors in the soup seem like they may be a hard sell for your picky eaters, try some of these tips to encourage them to sample the soup (and don't forget that it often takes several attempts to successfully introduce a new food). Tip One—Let the children pick the filled wontons out of the broth and eat those alone at first. Tip Two—Let your kids smell the fresh ginger as well as a jar of ground ginger. Ask them to compare the scents and tell you what the smells remind them of. Tip Three—Many kids who don't like cooked spinach love fresh spinach leaves. Try omitting the spinach from the broth and serving it as a side salad instead. They can roll up the spinach leaves and dip them in ranch dressing; adding a familiar, well-liked taste to a new meal often makes trying the new stuff easier.

FAMILY WONTON SOUP

½   pound ground pork, chicken, or turkey
½   cup finely chopped water chestnuts
4   tablespoons soy sauce, divided
2   egg whites, lightly beaten
2   teaspoons minced fresh ginger
24   wonton wrappers
2   49-ounce cans chicken broth
3   cups spinach leaves
2   cups thinly sliced cooked pork
1   cup chopped green onions
2   tablespoons dark sesame oil
1   carrot, shredded (optional)

COMBINE GROUND PORK, WATER CHESTNUTS, 2 tablespoons of the soy sauce, egg whites, and minced ginger in a medium bowl and mix well. Place 1 wonton wrapper on your work surface, with the bottom tip pointing toward the edge of the counter. Mound 1 teaspoon filling toward bottom tip. Fold bottom tip over filling, then roll wrapper over once. Moisten inside points with water. Bring side points together firmly to seal. Repeat with remaining wrappers and filling. Keep finished wontons covered with plastic wrap while filling remaining wrappers to help wrappers stay moist.

Combine broth and remaining 2 tablespoons soy sauce in a large pot. Bring the broth to a boil over high heat. Reduce the heat to medium and add the wontons. Simmer, uncovered, 4 minutes. Stir in the spinach, cooked pork and onions; immediately remove from heat. Stir in the dark sesame oil. Ladle soup into bowls. Sprinkle with a pinch of shredded carrots, if desired.

Serves 6.

CRUNCHY WONTON CHIPS

2 tablespoons soy sauce
1 tablespoon sesame or vegetable oil
1 teaspoon sugar
½ teaspoon garlic salt
24 wonton wrappers

PREHEAT OVEN TO 375 DEGREES. In a small bowl, combine soy sauce, oil, sugar, and garlic salt and mix well. Cut each wonton wrapper diagonally in half. Place wrappers on large cookie sheet that has been coated with non-stick cooking spray. Brush soy mixture lightly over both sides of skins with a pastry brush or your fingers. Bake 6 minutes or until crisp and lightly browned, turning after 3 minutes. Transfer to cooling rack; cool completely. Serve with Tasty Oriental Salsa.

Serves 6.

TASTY ORIENTAL SALSA

2	cups unpeeled, diced cucumber
1	cup chopped red bell pepper
1	cup chopped yellow or green bell pepper
1	cup yellow onion, chopped
1	cup fresh, coarsely chopped cilantro leaves
4	tablespoons soy sauce
2	tablespoons rice vinegar
2	tablespoons minced garlic
1	teaspoon dark sesame oil
¼ to ½	teaspoon red pepper flakes

COMBINE THE CUCUMBER, BELL PEPPERS, ONIONS, cilantro, soy sauce, rice vinegar, garlic, oil, and red pepper flakes in medium bowl until well blended. Cover and refrigerate until serving time.

Serves 4 to 6.

WEEK 33

I have many happy memories of going fishing with my dad. Once, instead of pulling the fish into the boat, the fish pulled me into the water! After dinner tonight, gather your family for a game of Go Fish! *Or perhaps you could even schedule a family fishing trip.*

GO FISH!

6   frozen tilapia fillets
½   cup low-fat mayonnaise
2   tablespoons lemon pepper

LAY THE FROZEN TILAPIA FILLETS ON A LARGE PLATE. With a butter knife, thinly spread mayonnaise onto fillets. Sprinkle lemon pepper evenly on top of fillets. Cover with plastic wrap and microwave on high power for 4 minutes. Serve while hot.

Serves 6.

BROCCOLI IN CREAMY CHEESE SAUCE

2   pounds broccoli, washed and cut into sections
1   8-ounce package cream cheese, softened
1   cup milk
1   teaspoon salt
½   teaspoon garlic salt
½   cup grated Parmesan cheese

PREHEAT OVEN TO 350 DEGREES. Beat softened cream cheese and milk together until creamy. Add salt, garlic salt, and cheese. Layer broccoli in the bottom of a 9x13-inch baking dish and spread creamy sauce over the top. Cover with aluminum foil and bake for 25 minutes.

Serves 6.

TWICE THE BAKED POTATO

6 to 8   large russet potatoes, washed and wrapped in foil
1   8-ounce package cream cheese, softened
1   cup sour cream
1   cup shredded cheddar cheese, divided
½   cup finely chopped green onions or chives
6   strips bacon, cooked crisp and crumbled

PREHEAT OVEN TO 400 DEGREES. Bake the potatoes on a cookie sheet for 1 hour or until soft. When done, let cool. Unwrap potatoes and cut in half from pole to pole. Spoon out insides into a medium bowl. Place shells back on cookie sheet and reduce oven temperature to 300 degrees. To the potatoes, add softened cream cheese, sour cream, ½ cup of the cheese, and green onion. Whip with an electric mixer until a nice mashed-potato texture forms. Spoon mixture back into empty skins. Top with bacon and remaining cheese. Bake, uncovered, for 40 minutes.

Serves 6 to 8.

BLACKBERRY CREAM PIE

1   9-inch graham cracker crumb pie shell
1   egg white, beaten
1   cup heavy cream
1   8-ounce package cream cheese, softened
1   10-ounce jar blackberry spread
1   pound fresh blackberries
    Mint leaves (optional), for garnish

PREHEAT OVEN TO 375 DEGREES. Brush pie shell with beaten egg white. Bake for 5 minutes. Cool on a wire rack. In a medium mixing bowl, beat whipping cream with an electric mixer until stiff peaks form; set aside. In a large mixing bowl beat cream cheese with an electric mixer on medium-high speed until smooth. Add blackberry spread and beat on low speed just until combined. Fold in whipped cream. Spoon mixture into pie shell. Cover and freeze for 4 hours or overnight. When ready to serve, spread fresh blackberries on top and/or mint leaves with some extra whipped cream, if desired.

Serves 6 to 8.

WEEK 34

The most enjoyable times in life are those spent with others, doing small and simple things. As summer winds to an end, try this week's simple but tasty recipes, which can be prepared quickly so you and the kids can spend a late-summer evening playing together. Heat up the grill and hit the backyard for this fun family barbecue. We like to finish off this meal by eating over-sized root beer floats as the sun sets.

HERBED CHICKEN KABOBS

1	envelope dry onion soup mix
½	cup water
2	tablespoons olive oil
½	teaspoon dried thyme
½	teaspoon ground black pepper
½	teaspoon garlic powder
1	pound boneless, skinless chicken breasts, cut into 1-inch pieces
1	green pepper, cut into 1-inch squares
1	red pepper, cut into 1-inch squares
1	6-ounce package sliced pepperoni
1	6-ounce package Canadian bacon rounds

COMBINE FIRST 6 INGREDIENTS IN A LARGE BOWL. Add chicken pieces, pepperoni slices, and Canadian bacon rounds. Chill at least 1 hour. Remove meat mixture, reserving the marinade. Thread chicken, peppers, pepperoni, and Canadian bacon onto 6 10-inch skewers. Grill kabobs directly above medium coals or medium gas heat, for about 10 to 15 minutes, until chicken is no longer pink. Turn frequently, brushing with marinade each time.

Serves 6.

GRILLED CORN ON THE COB

8   ears fresh corn on the cob, husked and washed
    Butter, melted
    Seasoned salt

WASH AND HUSK THE CORN. Make a boat with a 12-inch piece of aluminum foil and lay the corn inside. Brush with melted butter and seasoned salt. Grill for about 10 minutes over medium coals or medium gas heat, turning corn inside of boat often, so all sides are grilled evenly. Serve hot.

Serves 8.

SWEET BAKED BEANS

2   28-ounce cans pork and beans
1   cup your favorite barbecue sauce
2   tablespoons maple-flavored syrup
4   slices bacon, sliced in half and partially cooked

PREHEAT OVEN TO 350 DEGREES. In a 2-quart casserole dish, combine pork and beans, barbecue sauce, and syrup. Arrange bacon on top of beans. Bake for 1 hour or until hot and bubbling.

Serves 6 to 8.

WEEK 35

There are probably 101 ways to make enchiladas. This week's main dish has got to be one of the easiest. This is a great dish to prepare during the weeks when the kids are heading back to school and the family is busy settling into a new routine. Because the dish is easy, you'll have more time to sit around the table and talk about the new school year. Serve with fresh pineapple spears and a bagged green salad.

ENCHILADA CASSEROLE

1	cup sour cream
2	10.75-ounce cans cream of chicken soup
1	4.5-ounce can chopped green chilies
1	4.25-ounce can sliced olives
1½	pounds ground beef
1	teaspoon salt
1	teaspoon ground black pepper
1	teaspoon garlic salt
½	large yellow or sweet onion, chopped
1	16-ounce can refried beans
2	teaspoons minced garlic
2	teaspoons dried oregano
1	teaspoon dried basil
1	tablespoon cumin
½	cup fresh, chopped cilantro leaves
1	10-ounce can enchilada sauce
12	10-inch flour tortillas
1	pound mild cheddar cheese, shredded

PREHEAT OVEN TO 350 DEGREES. Combine sour cream, soup, green chilies, and olives in a large bowl; set aside. In a large skillet over medium heat, brown ground beef with salt, pepper, garlic salt, onion, beans, garlic, oregano, basil, cumin, and fresh cilantro. Pour ½ of the enchilada sauce in a 9x13-inch baking dish; set aside. Bring a large pot of water to a boil. Dip flour tortillas, one at a time, in boiling water for just an instant to soften them. Pat dry with a paper towel. Fill the tortillas with 1 large tablespoon sour cream mixture, 1 large tablespoon meat mixture, and a handful of cheese. Fill all 12 tortillas and fold in sides. Roll up and place, seam side down, in casserole dish. Put remaining sour cream mixture on top of filled tortillas and the rest of the enchilada sauce. Top with remaining cheese. Bake for 35 minutes.

Serves 6 to 8.

Granny's Fruit Salad

      2   cups whipping cream
      1   cup pineapple chunks or tidbits, drained
      1   cup mandarin orange segments, drained
      1   cup flaked coconut
      1   cup miniature marshmallows
      ½   cup sour cream

Beat the whipping cream until light and fluffy. Combine all ingredients in a large bowl. Chill until ready to serve.

Serves 6.

WEEK 36

This week's recipes remind me of home, of playing in the mud with my brother and testing out my aim—and my mud pies—on him. We'd play all afternoon, until Mom called us in to dinner and served up a meal much like the one here. Create similar memories for your children by bringing this tasty casserole and dish full of potato volcanoes to your table. Your kids will never forget it.

YUMMY TATER TOT CASSEROLE

1   pound ground beef
1   small onion, chopped
1   teaspoon dried basil
1   teaspoon seasoned salt
2   5-ounce cans evaporated milk
2   10.75-ounce cans cream of chicken soup
1   32-ounce bag frozen Tater Tots®
1   cup shredded cheddar cheese

PREHEAT OVEN TO 350 DEGREES. Brown the ground beef and the onion together in a large sauce pan or skillet over medium-high heat. Add the basil and seasoned salt. Stir in canned milk and soup. Coat a 9x13-inch baking dish with nonstick cooking spray. Spread the soup mixture in the bottom of the dish. Spread Tater Tots over the top of the soup mixture. Sprinkle cheese over this. Bake for 30 minutes.

Serves 6 to 8.

Idaho Volcanoes

6   large russet potatoes, peeled and cubed
4   tablespoons butter, divided
1   teaspoon salt
1   tablespoon sugar
½   cup, plus 1 tablespoon, evaporated milk
2   egg yolks
¾   cup grated American cheese

Preheat oven to 350 degrees. Cover cubed potatoes with water in a large pot. Bring water to a boil, reduce heat, cover, and simmer until potatoes are fork tender, about 15 to 20 minutes. Drain off water. Mash potatoes slightly with a fork or potato masher. Add 2 tablespoons of the butter, the salt, sugar, and ½ cup of the evaporated milk. Beat until light and fluffy. In a baking dish, shape potatoes into cones about 3 inches high. Make a deep indentation in the top of each potato cone. In a mixing bowl, combine egg yolks, remaining butter, remaining 1 tablespoon evaporated milk, and grated cheese. Mix well. Fill cones with cheese mixture and bake in oven for about 10 to 15 minutes, until cheese melts and starts to brown and run over down the sides.

If you want to make 1 large volcano cone, bake in 450-degree oven until cheese mixture puffs up and starts to run down the sides.

Serves 6.

NOT-YOUR-USUAL-GREEN-BEAN-CASSEROLE

3   14.5-ounce cans green beans, drained
3   slices American cheese
1   10.75-ounce can cream of mushroom soup
1   tablespoon Worcestershire sauce
1   teaspoon ground black pepper
1   tablespoon lemon juice
2   cups dry bread crumbs

PREHEAT OVEN TO 350 DEGREES. Coat a 9x13-inch baking dish with non-stick cooking spray.

Pour the green beans into the baking dish. Place cheese slices on beans. In a small bowl, mix the soup, Worcestershire sauce, pepper, and lemon juice. Pour sauce over the cheese and top with bread crumbs. Bake for 30 minutes.

Serves 6 to 8.

WEEK 37

Kids love hot dogs, so this week's meal is sure to please. Couple the dish with light and fluffy Parmesan Biscuits and finish off with a bowl of simple vanilla ice cream. Delicious!

FRANK FIESTA

1	tablespoon vegetable oil
10	hot dogs, cut diagonally into ½-inch pieces
1	medium onion, chopped
1	15-ounce can tomato sauce
1	cup canned whole kernel corn
1	cup water
1	teaspoon chili powder
½	green pepper, chopped
1	cup canned kidney beans, drained and rinsed
4	cups uncooked spiral macaroni or wide egg noodles
1	teaspoon salt

HEAT OIL IN A LARGE SKILLET OVER MEDIUM HEAT. Sauté hot dog slices and onion in oil until hot dogs are light brown and onion is tender. Stir in remaining ingredients. Heat to boiling; reduce heat. Cover and simmer, stirring occasionally, until macaroni is tender. About 20 to 25 minutes.

Serves 6.

Parmesan Biscuits

2	cups all-purpose flour
1	tablespoon sugar
4	teaspoons baking powder
½	teaspoon salt
½	cup shortening
1	egg
⅔	cup milk
½	cup butter, melted
½	cup grated Parmesan cheese

Preheat oven to 450 degrees. Whisk dry ingredients together in a medium mixing bowl. Cut the shortening into the flour mixture with a fork or pastry cutter until it forms coarse crumbs the size of a pea. Combine egg and milk in a small bowl. Mix well, and add to the flour mixture. Stir with a fork until it clings together. Turn dough out onto a floured surface and knead 1 minute. Using a rolling pin, roll out to about ¾-inch thickness. Use a biscuit cutter or a round glass to cut dough into biscuits. Gather dough scraps into a ball and roll out again to make more biscuits. Roll each biscuit in melted butter. Put Parmesan cheese in a small bowl and roll buttered biscuit in cheese. Put biscuits on a large cookie sheet and bake for 10 to 12 minutes.

Serves 6 to 8.

WEEK 38

As the weather grows cooler, warm, home-cooked meals provide just the comfort your family needs. This week, introduce them to a new kind of pie, coupled with light, fluffy biscuits. Mmm.

SHEPHERD'S PIE

3	cups instant mashed potato buds
2⅓	cups milk
4	tablespoons butter
2	teaspoons salt, divided
1	cup sour cream
1	tablespoon chopped garlic
1	pound ground beef
1	teaspoon ground black pepper
1	12-ounce jar beef gravy, or 2 packets beef gravy mix and 2 cups water, mixed well
1	15.25-ounce can corn, drained
1	14.5-ounce can green beans, drained
1	14.5-ounce can carrots, drained
1	cup grated Parmesan or cheddar cheese

PREHEAT OVEN TO 350 DEGREES. Prepare mashed potatoes according to package directions, using the 3 cups buds, 2⅓ cups milk, 4 tablespoons butter, and 1 teaspoon salt listed above. Fold in the sour cream and garlic; set aside. In a large skillet, brown ground beef over medium-high heat, seasoning with the remaining teaspoon salt and the pepper. Do not drain fat off meat. Stir in gravy and canned vegetables. Cook over medium heat until heated through. Layer in a 9x13-inch glass dish or baking pan, beginning with the meat and vegetable mixture, followed by the mashed potatoes, and finally, the cheese. Cover with aluminum foil and bake 30 minutes.

Serves 6 to 8.

CLOUD BISCUITS

½ cup shortening
4 cups all-purpose flour
⅔ cup sugar
1 teaspoon salt
4 teaspoons baking powder
2 eggs
¾ cup milk or buttermilk
¼ cup mayonnaise

PREHEAT OVEN TO 400 DEGREES. In a large bowl, cut shortening into flour with a knife or pastry cutter until it resembles coarse crumbs the size of a pea. Add remaining ingredients and mix well until dough forms. Flour your hands lightly, reach in, and knead dough 6 times until smooth. Dust your clean countertop with some flour. Using a rolling pin, roll dough to 1½-inch thickness. Using a cup or a circle cookie cutter, cut biscuits and place on a cookie sheet coated with nonstick cooking spray. Gather together dough scraps, shape into a ball, and roll out. Repeat until the dough is gone. Bake for 10 minutes, until golden brown. Put a clean towel in a basket or pretty bowl and place hot biscuits inside. Cover to keep warm.

This recipe is good with honey butter (1 stick softened butter whipped with 1 cup honey) or a homemade raspberry jam.

Makes 2 dozen biscuits.

WEEK 39

Homemade stew doesn't have to take all day to make. You can save time by using canned roast beef and broth. If you wouldn't think of buying canned meat at the store, you can still make this week's dish with fresh stew meat from the butcher's counter. The recipe is easy enough that you'll save time no matter what method you choose. The smell will definitely lure the kids into the kitchen, where they probably won't even notice that it's chock full of veggies. I like to serve a fresh grape and strawberry fruit salad, mixed with some poppy seed dressing, as a compliment to this meal.

BUSY HOMEMAKER'S STEW

2   12-ounce cans roast beef with gravy, or 1½ pounds stew meat

6   cups beef broth, divided

1   cup diced celery

¾   cup chopped carrots

3   medium russet potatoes, peeled and diced

¼   cup minced dry onions

1   14.5-ounce can green beans, undrained

1   14.5-ounce can diced tomatoes

2   tablespoons red wine vinegar

1   tablespoon lemon juice

1   teaspoon dried basil

1   tablespoon seasoned salt

1   teaspoon ground black pepper

3   tablespoons all-purpose flour

IF USING FRESH STEW MEAT, heat 2 tablespoons oil in a large pot over medium-high heat. Add stew meat and brown on all sides, about 5 minutes. If using canned roast beef, pour contents of cans into the large soup pot. Remaining directions are identical, regardless of meat used.

Reserve 1 cup of the beef broth, then add remaining ingredients, with the exception of the flour, to the soup pot. Bring to a boil over medium-high heat, reduce heat to a simmer, cover, and cook until potatoes and carrots are almost tender, about 12 minutes. Whisk flour into reserved 1 cup beef broth until all lumps are removed. Gently stir flour mixture into simmering stew. Return to a gentle rolling boil and simmer for another 10 minutes. If using fresh stew meat, ensure that meat is cooked through before serving; it may require additional cooking time.

Serves 6.

CORN FRITTERS

    1   14.75-ounce can cream-style corn
    2   cups all-purpose flour
    ½   teaspoon salt
    2   eggs
    4   teaspoons baking powder
    2   tablespoons sugar
        Canola oil

COMBINE CREAM-STYLE CORN, FLOUR, SALT, eggs, baking powder, and sugar in a medium bowl to make a sweet, sticky dough. Heat 2 inches oil in a large saucepan over medium heat. Drop dough by spoonfuls into hot cooking oil. Cook until golden brown. Take out with tongs and lay on a plate lined with paper towels. Serve with butter and honey or dip in stew.

Serves 6.

WEEK 40

This week, try out a comforting homemade soup served in bread bowls. Children will love the idea that they can eat their bowls, which will encourage them to try something new. If desired, the soup can be made in advance and frozen for up to 4 months. This meal goes well with green or red grapes or another of your kids' favorite fruits.

CREAMY POTATO SOUP

3	14-ounce cans beef broth
1	cup minced onion
1	cup chopped celery
5	potatoes, peeled and diced
2	large carrots, peeled and chopped
4	cups cream or milk (cream works best)
½	cup butter
½	cup all-purpose flour
¼	cup white cooking wine
2	teaspoons seasoned salt
¼	cup chopped Italian parsley
	Grated Parmesan or cheddar cheese, for garnish

IN A LARGE SOUP POT, BRING BROTH TO A BOIL over medium-high heat. Add onion, celery, potatoes, and carrots. Boil, covered, for about 10 minutes, until vegetables are tender. Stir in the cream. In a separate bowl, melt butter in the microwave on high power. Add flour and stir to make a roux. Once roux is mixed well, add slowly to hot soup, stirring vigorously with a wire whisk until roux is gone. Bring to a slow rolling boil over medium heat. Soup will thicken to a nice creamy texture. Add cooking wine, seasoned salt, and parsley. Let simmer for about 20 minutes. Garnish with grated cheese.

Serves 8 to 10.

French Bread Soup Bowls

2½ cups warm water
3 tablespoons sugar
2 packages dry active yeast
1 tablespoon salt
5 tablespoons oil
6 cups all-purpose flour

Preheat oven to 400 degrees. In a large bowl or the bowl of an electric bread mixer, combine warm water and sugar. Sprinkle yeast over the top and stir. Wait 10 minutes until yeast mixture is frothy. Add salt, oil, and half of the flour. Beat well in mixer or with a wooden spoon. Add remaining flour and mix well until a soft dough forms. Turn dough out onto a floured board and knead 2 or 3 times to coat with flour. Divide into 8 to 10 equal parts, depending on size of bowls desired. Form into large balls and place in small foil pans (small pot pie pans work well). Allow dough bowls to rise for 20 minutes. Bake for 25 minutes or until lightly browned. Remove from pans. Cut off tops and hollow out insides. Serve with soup.

Makes 8 to 10 bread bowls.

WEEK 41

This week, try out some fun recipes that you probably haven't always associated with dinner. Your kids will get a kick out of the recipe names and have a great time helping prepare the somewhat whacky dishes. These might also make a great menu for a children's party.

LITTLE BURTS

2   14-ounce packages mini cocktail franks, such as Hillshire Farm® Lit'l Beef Franks® or Lit'l Smokies®
2   19-ounce bottles your favorite barbecue sauce

PLACE COCKTAIL FRANKS IN A SLOW COOKER and pour barbecue sauce over the top. Set the cooker to low and let the franks simmer for a couple of hours or through the day.

Serves 8 to 10.

BRAINS WITH CHEESE

1   head cauliflower
½   cup water
1   teaspoon seasoned salt
1   10.75-ounce can Campbell's® Cheddar Cheese Soup

RINSE OFF HEAD OF CAULIFLOWER, remove green leaves, and place in a medium-sized, microwaveable bowl. Add water and sprinkle cauliflower with seasoned salt. Pour cheese soup over cauliflower to cover. Cover with plastic wrap and microwave on high power for 4 minutes. Serve hot.

Serves 6.

Double-Layer Pumpkin Pie

4	ounces cream cheese, softened
1	tablespoon half-and-half (milk also works)
1½	cups Cool Whip®, thawed
1	store-bought graham cracker crumb pie crust
1	cup milk
2	3-ounce packages vanilla instant pudding
1	16-ounce can pumpkin
1	teaspoon ground cinnamon
½	teaspoon ground ginger
¼	teaspoon ground cloves

Mix cream cheese, half-and-half, and sugar in a bowl with a wire whisk until smooth. Stir in whipped topping and spread mixture over graham cracker crust; set aside. Pour 1 cup milk into a medium bowl, add pudding mixes, and beat with whisk for 1 minute. Mixture will be quite thick. Stir in pumpkin and spices with wire whisk until well mixed. Spread over cream cheese layer. Chill in refrigerator for 4 hours, until set. If desired, garnish with additional whipped topping and sprinkle lightly with a little nutmeg.

Serves 6 to 8.

WEEK 42

These recipes are perfect for a fun fall or Halloween gathering with friends and family. Depending on the crowd, double or triple the recipes to meet your needs.

BAT WINGS

1	cup apricot jam
¼	cup crystallized ginger, or 3 tablespoons chopped fresh ginger
3	teaspoons chopped garlic
1	teaspoon salt
¼	cup white wine vinegar
4	pounds chicken wings

IF YOU DON'T PLAN TO MARINATE THE CHICKEN, preheat oven to 450 degrees.

Line a large cake pan or jelly roll pan with aluminum foil. Coat foil with nonstick cooking spray. Place wings in prepared pan and set aside. In a food processor, combine jam, ginger, garlic, and salt. Blend until well-mixed. Stir in vinegar. You should have more than 1 cup of glaze. For a stronger taste, pour glaze over wings and marinate for 3 hours. If you are in a hurry, brush chicken with glaze and roast immediately for 15 minutes. Remove pan from oven and turn wings over with tongs. Brush wings with glaze that has settled in the bottom of the pan, return to oven, and roast an additional 15 minutes. If wings have been marinating in the sauce, let cold pan come to room temperature and brush wings liberally with sauce that has settled in the pan before roasting.

Serves 6 to 8.

Green Salad by the Layers

1	head iceberg or green leaf lettuce, washed and chopped
1	16-ounce bag spinach, washed and chopped
3	stalks celery, diced
½	cup chopped green pepper
1	green onion, chopped
1½	cups frozen peas
1	4.5-ounce can sliced water chestnuts
1	cup mayonnaise
1	cup sour cream
2	tablespoons grated Parmesan cheese
3	tablespoons sugar
1	teaspoon garlic salt
1	cup shredded cheddar cheese
2	tomatoes, chopped
¼	pound bacon, cooked crisp and crumbled

LAYER, IN THIS ORDER, THE LETTUCE, SPINACH, celery, green pepper, onion, peas, and water chestnuts in a 9x13-inch glass baking dish or a decorative glass bowl or trifle dish.

In a small bowl, combine mayonnaise, sour cream, Parmesan cheese, sugar, and garlic salt. Spread dressing evenly on top of the salad. Top with cheese, tomatoes, and bacon.

Serves 6.

EASY, BUTTERY BREADSTICKS

½   cup butter, melted
½   cup freshly grated Parmesan cheese
24   Rhodes® Frozen Dinner Rolls, thawed but still cold*
    Garlic salt

POUR MELTED BUTTER IN A DEEP-DISH plate or a pie tin. Place cheese in another pie tin or deep-dish plate. Roll each dough ball into a 6-inch long rope. Dredge each piece in melted butter, then cheese to coat. Place breadsticks on a baking sheet in 2 vertical rows. Sprinkle with garlic salt. Cover with plastic wrap sprayed with nonstick cooking spray. Let rise in a warm, draft-free place until double in size. Remove plastic wrap and bake at 350 degrees for 10 to 15 minutes or until golden brown.

Makes 24 breadsticks.

You can speed up the process by thawing the frozen roll dough in the microwave for 2 minutes on high power. The dough should be soft and pliable but still cool. Then follow the recipe as written above. Breadsticks will double in size in about 35 minutes.

YUMMY PUMPKIN BARS

4   eggs
2   cups sugar
1   cup oil
1   15-ounce can pumpkin
2   teaspoons ground cinnamon
2   cups all-purpose flour
2   teaspoons baking soda
½   teaspoon salt
1   3-ounce package cream cheese, softened

1   teaspoon vanilla
1   tablespoon milk or cream
6   tablespoons butter, softened
3   cups powdered sugar
    dash of salt

PREHEAT OVEN TO 350 DEGREES. Spray a 9x13-inch baking dish with non-stick cooking spray; set aside.

In a large bowl, beat eggs with an electric mixer until frothy. Add sugar, oil, and pumpkin; mix until smooth. Add cinnamon, flour, baking soda, and salt. Spread evenly in prepared pan and bake 25 to 30 minutes. Cake is done when a wooden toothpick inserted in center comes out clean. Cool completely on a wire rack.

Prepare frosting by mixing cream cheese, vanilla, milk or cream, butter, powdered sugar, and a dash of salt in a medium bowl until smooth. Frost cake and cut into squares.

Makes 18 to 24 squares.

WEEK 43

This recipe is delicious and a creative way to hide the servings of fruits and vegetables. For tonight's dinner, turn your dining room into a Mexican restaurant. Have the kids wear nametags with their names written in Spanish or teach them how to say "please" and "thank you" in Spanish.

BLACK BEAN AND CITRUS PORK TACOS WITH AVOCADO-ORANGE SALSA

2	pounds pork
2	15-ounce cans vegetable broth
4	ripe medium avocados, chopped
2	small oranges, peeled and chopped
½	cup chopped red onion
½	cup fresh, chopped cilantro leaves
2	15-ounce cans black beans, drained and rinsed
2	teaspoons cumin
2	tablespoons freshly squeezed lime juice
2	boxes corn taco shells
4	cups shredded cheddar-Monterey Jack cheese blend

PLACE PORK IN 4-QUART SLOW COOKER and cover with vegetable broth. Cook on low for 8 hours. With two forks, shred pork.

Heat oven to 350 degrees. Peel, pit, and chop avocados. To prepare avocado salsa, gently toss avocados, oranges, onions, and cilantro in a small bowl until mixed. Cover and set aside.

Combine black beans, cumin, and lime juice in a medium saucepan. Bring to a boil and then simmer for 10 minutes. Place taco shells on a large cookie sheet. Divide bean mixture evenly among shells. Sprinkle with cheese. Bake 6 to 8 minutes or until cheese is melted. Remove taco shells from the oven and add pork to each shell. Top with avocado salsa.

Serves 6 to 8.

STRAWBERRY MOUSSE

   1¼   cup strawberries
   ¼   cup cold water
   1   1-ounce package unflavored gelatin
   ¼   cup boiling water
   1   teaspoon lemon zest
   ⅓   cup sugar
   1½   cups heavy cream
   4   mint leaves

SET ASIDE 6 LARGE STRAWBERRIES FOR THE GARNISH. Wash and remove stems from the rest of the strawberries.

Pour cold water into a small bowl and sprinkle with gelatin. Let stand for 2 minutes. Pour boiling water over the gelatin mixture and whisk until gelatin is dissolved.

Pour the gelatin mixture into a blender; add strawberries, lemon zest, and sugar and puree until smooth. Whip the cream with an electric mixer until it forms soft peaks; set aside a few dollops for garnish. Gently fold the strawberry-gelatin mixture into the whipped cream. Spoon the mousse into parfait or stemmed glasses, cover, and refrigerate for at least 3 hours. Just before serving, garnish each glass with reserved whipped cream, strawberries, and mint leaves.

Serves 4 to 6.

WEEK 44

These are two of my favorite recipes. The tempura is "deceptively delicious" and disguises those vegetables your kids may be wary of trying. You could try eating dinner with different cooking utensils or wearing gloves. Creating fun memories is what life is all about.

GORGEOUS PORK CHOPS IN SAUCE

2	cups salad croutons
2	eggs
6	bone-in pork chops, about 1-inch thick
1	8-ounce tub onion and chive cream cheese
½	cup chicken broth
4	tablespoons milk

PREHEAT OVEN TO 350 DEGREES. Coat a 9x13-inch baking dish with non-stick cooking spray.

Pour croutons into a large Ziploc bag. Crush with a cup or a rolling pin. Once crushed, transfer to a shallow bowl. In a second shallow bowl, beat eggs. Dip pork chops first in the egg and then in the crouton crumbs, making sure each chop is completely covered. Place chops in prepared baking dish and bake for about 40 minutes. Meanwhile, in a medium saucepan combine cream cheese, chicken broth, and milk. Cook over medium heat for 5 minutes and stir until smooth and blended. Serve over pork chops.

Serves 6.

VEGETABLE TEMPURA

6 to 8   cups mixed vegetables (broccoli, sweet potatoes, mushrooms, carrots, cauliflower, onion, green or red peppers, zucchini, scallions, snow peas, green beans, turnips)
1   cup flour
⅓   cup cornstarch
3   teaspoons baking powder
1   teaspoon salt
1   egg white
1½   cup water, divided
    Vegetable oil, for frying
    Soy sauce, Oriental hot sauce, or ranch dressing, for dipping

RINSE THE VEGETABLES AND CUT INTO BITE-SIZED PIECES. (For example, cut carrots and scallions on the diagonal; cut sweet potatoes into strips; cut mushrooms in half.)

Mix the flour, cornstarch, baking powder, and salt in a large bowl. In a smaller bowl, whisk the egg white and 1 cup of the water until just combined. Gradually stir the egg mixture into the dry ingredients until barely blended. The batter should be thin and lumpy. Add more water, if needed.

Fill a large frying pan 1-inch deep with vegetable oil and warm over medium-high heat. Dip the vegetables into the batter, tapping off any excess. Set the pieces one by one into the hot oil and fry on both sides until golden, about 2 to 4 minutes. Keep vegetables separate so they don't stick together.

Drain the pieces on paper towels and move to a cookie sheet. Place cookie sheet in a warm oven until all the vegetables are fried. Place vegetables on a platter with soy sauce, hot sauce, or ranch dressing for dipping.

Serves 4.

WEEK 45

This week's recipes are perfect for the holiday season and are some of my family's favorite dishes. A big thanks to my friend Janet, whose cranberry sauce is to die for. Thank you for letting me share it!

THANKSGIVING TURKEY

1	10-pound turkey, thawed
2	14-ounce cans chicken broth
1	10.5-ounce can turkey gravy
¼	cup butter, melted
2	tablespoons Worcestershire sauce
4	tablespoons all-purpose flour
5	slices bacon
1	teaspoon garlic pepper
2	teaspoons dried sage
2	teaspoons poultry seasoning
2	teaspoons seasoned salt
1	teaspoon lemon pepper

PREHEAT OVEN TO 250 DEGREES. Open up turkey and clean out gizzards and innards. Rinse off turkey with cold water and pat dry; set aside. Whisk together chicken broth, gravy, butter, Worcestershire sauce, and flour until no lumps remain. Pour mixture into a large roasting pan. Place turkey in the roaster. Lay bacon strips across the top of the turkey to cover it. Sprinkle the spices across the top of the bacon. Cover with aluminum foil and the roasting pan lid. Place roaster in oven and cook turkey for 8 hours.

Serves 10.

Janet's Best Cranberry Relish

1   orange; seeds, peel, and pith removed
1   large red delicious apple, cored but unpeeled
3   cups sugar
3   16-ounce bags fresh cranberries
    Juice of half a lemon

Cut orange into 8 sections. Cut apple into sections. Process orange in a blender or food processor until fine. Add the sections of apple and sugar. Blend until fine. Add fresh cranberries and lemon juice. Blend until well mixed but not too fine. Refrigerate a few hours to blend flavors. Save what you need for a holiday meal and freeze the rest to eat with leftover turkey.

Serves 10.

Sausage Appetizer

16   ounces Jimmy Dean® Regular Pork Sausage
1   7-ounce jar green chili salsa
1   4.5-ounce can diced green chilies
1   8-ounce package cream cheese, softened
1   cup sour cream
    Water crackers, or your favorite cracker, for serving

Brown the sausage in a medium skillet over medium heat. In a medium-sized mixing bowl, combine all other ingredients except crackers; add browned sausage and mix well. Chill until ready to serve. Serve with water crackers or crackers of your choice.

Serves 8 to 10.

Apple Presents

1   teaspoon orange zest
½   cup sugar
½   teaspoon ground cinnamon
⅓   cup freshly squeezed orange juice
2   medium Granny Smith apples, peeled, cored, and sliced
1   11-ounce tube refrigerated bread stick dough
1   tablespoon butter, melted

Preheat oven to 375 degrees. In a small bowl, combine zest, sugar, and cinnamon; set aside. Pour orange juice in the bottom of a deep-dish plate or glass pan. Unroll refrigerator dough and separate at perforations to form 12 strips. Place 3 to 4 apple slices at the end of each strip of dough and roll up. Place in prepared pan. Brush melted butter over the presents and then sprinkle with cinnamon-zest mixture. Bake 25 to 30 minutes, or until golden brown.

Serves 6 to 8.

WEEK 46

Here is a tasty soup recipe and some delicious dippers. Have fun this week by inviting the children to create their own menus using imaginary foods. Encourage them to describe the look and flavor of their fantasy foods.

TASTY TACO SOUP

2   16-ounce cans traditional refried beans
2   10-ounce cans Ro*Tel® Mexican Festival diced tomatoes with lime and cilantro, undrained
2   cups chicken broth
1   cup coconut milk
1   envelope taco seasoning mix
    Sour cream, for garnish
    Shredded cheddar cheese, for garnish
    Fresh, chopped cilantro leaves, for garnish

STIR REFRIED BEANS, TOMATOES, BROTH, coconut milk, and taco seasoning mix in a medium saucepan; heat to boiling. Reduce heat to low and simmer, uncovered, for about 20 minutes.

Garnish with sour cream, cheddar cheese, and cilantro.

Serves 8 to 10.

CRISPY TAQUITO DIPPERS

       12   sticks sharp cheddar cheese
       24   10-inch flour tortillas
        2   tablespoons vegetable oil

PREHEAT OVEN TO 350 DEGREES. Cut each cheese stick in half lengthwise to make 2 thin sticks. Place 1 thin stick on edge of each tortilla; roll tortilla tightly around cheese. Brush edge of tortilla with water to seal. Press to seal. Repeat with remaining cheese and tortillas. Place taquitos, seam sides down, on cookie sheet. Brush each lightly with oil. Bake 5 to 7 minutes or until edges of tortillas are golden brown and cheese is melted. Serve with Tasty Taco Soup.

Serves 6.

WEEK 47

Kids love silly jokes. Share this one over dinner: One day, Bart was walking along the road and met his friend Billy, who was holding a bag. "Hey, Billy," said Bart. "What's in the bag?" Billy replied, "Chickens." Bart said, "Chickens! Say, if I guess how many chickens you have in your bag, will you give me one?" Billy nodded. "Sure, Bart. If you guess how many chickens I have, I'll give you BOTH of 'em." Bart thought for a minute then guessed, "Five?"

"SWEET CHICKEN" AND NOODLES

12 ounces fresh, uncooked Chinese egg noodles
½ cup apricot preserves
6 tablespoons rice wine vinegar
3 tablespoons soy sauce
2 tablespoons cornstarch
2 tablespoons peanut, sesame, or vegetable oil, divided
1 red onion, thinly sliced
4 cups carrots, diagonally sliced
4 boneless, skinless chicken breasts, cut into thin strips
4 medium apricots, pitted and sliced into bite-sized pieces

COOK NOODLES ACCORDING TO PACKAGE DIRECTIONS, omitting salt. Drain and keep warm. Stir together apricot preserves, rice wine vinegar, soy sauce, and cornstarch; set aside. Heat 1 tablespoon of the oil in a large nonstick skillet or wok. Add onion and cook 2 minutes or until softened. Add carrots and cook 3 minutes. Remove vegetables to a medium bowl. Heat remaining oil in skillet. Add chicken and cook over medium-high heat 20 to 30 minutes, or until no longer pink. Push chicken to one side of skillet. Stir sauce and then add to skillet. Cook and stir until thick and bubbly. Coat chicken with sauce. Stir in vegetables and apricots; coat evenly. Cook

3 minutes or until heated through. Toss with noodles and serve immediately.

Serves 4 to 6.

LEMON BUTTERED GINGERBREAD

2¼	cups all-purpose flour
¾	cup sugar
2	teaspoons ground cinnamon
½	teaspoon ground nutmeg
¼	teaspoon ground cloves
1	teaspoon baking powder
1	teaspoon ground ginger
½	teaspoon baking soda
½	teaspoon salt
¾	cup water
¾	cup vegetable oil
¾	cup dark molasses
2	eggs
	Powdered sugar

PREHEAT OVEN TO 350 DEGREES. Grease a 9x13-inch glass baking dish.

Combine flour, the ¾ cup sugar, cinnamon, nutmeg, cloves, baking powder, ginger, baking soda, and salt, in a large mixing bowl. Stir in water, oil, molasses, and eggs; beat with electric mixer for 3 minutes. Pour into prepared dish. Bake for 35 to 40 minutes or until wooden toothpick inserted near center comes out clean.

Just before serving, dust with powdered sugar. Cut into squares or wedges and serve while still warm.

Serves 10.

WEEK 48

I love chili, especially on cold winter nights. It warms the heart and the soul. In addition to this week's chili recipe, try out the Sweet Corn Bread with Honey Butter and the delightful Lemonade Apples. You'll feel warmed through and through.

WINTER TACO CHILI

1 pound lean ground beef
1 medium onion, chopped
1 15-ounce can kidney beans, drained and rinsed
1 15-ounce can black beans, drained and rinsed
1 14.5-ounce can diced tomatoes, or 3 fresh tomatoes, diced
1 14.5-ounce can diced tomatoes with green chilies
1 15-ounce can tomato sauce
2 tablespoons lemon or lime juice
2 tablespoons red wine vinegar
2 teaspoons seasoned salt
2 teaspoons minced garlic
1 teaspoon chili powder
2 teaspoons dried Italian seasoning
1 15.25-ounce can corn
¼ cup chopped, fresh cilantro leaves
   Tortilla chips
   Grated cheddar cheese
   Sour cream

IN A LARGE POT OR DUTCH OVEN, brown ground beef and onion over medium heat. Stir in beans, tomatoes, and tomato sauce. Add lemon juice, red wine vinegar, seasoned salt, garlic, chili powder, Italian seasoning, and corn. Bring it all to a good rolling boil, then simmer for 20 to 30 minutes. Stir in cilantro. Serve topped with tortilla chips and grated cheese. Garnish with sour cream.

Serves 6 to 12.

SWEET CORN BREAD WITH HONEY BUTTER

½   cup all-purpose flour
4   teaspoons baking powder
1½ teaspoons salt
½   cup cornmeal
⅔   cup sugar
½   cup shortening
2½ cups milk
2   eggs
½   cup butter, softened
1   cup honey

PREHEAT OVEN TO 400 DEGREES. Spray a 9 x 13-inch baking dish with non-stick cooking spray, or line a standard muffin tin with 12 paper cups.

In a medium-sized mixing bowl, add flour, baking powder, salt, cornmeal, sugar, and shortening. Cut the shortening into the flour mixture until it resembles coarse crumbs about the size of a pea. Add milk and eggs and beat with an electric mixer until batter is smooth. Spread batter in prepared pan or muffin tins. Bake 20 to 30 minutes in a 9 x 13 pan or 20 to 25 minutes in the muffin tin. Cool slightly on wire rack while preparing honey butter.

To prepare honey butter, whip softened butter and honey in a small bowl with an electric beater until light and fluffy. Serve with warm bread or muffins.

Serves 12.

LEMONADE APPLES

6   Granny Smith or Braeburn apples, peeled, cored, and sliced

2   tablespoons sugar

3   tablespoons lemon juice, bottled or fresh

IN A MEDIUM BOWL, MIX SLICED APPLES, sugar, and lemon or lime juice. Chill until ready to serve.

This also makes a great kid-friendly snack. Put prepared apples in Ziploc bags and refrigerate for a healthy, but sweet snack.

Serves 6.

WEEK 49

These recipes are so yummy and easy to make. For the classic cheese fondue meal, pull out some of your old clothes from high school and let the kids come to dinner dressed up in them.

SOUTHWESTERN STUFFED CHICKEN

1   8-ounce tub onion and chives cream cheese spread
1   teaspoon garlic powder
1   teaspoon seasoned salt
1   cup canned whole kernel corn
8   taco shells, coarsely broken
1   teaspoon chili powder
6   boneless, skinless chicken breasts
3   tablespoons butter, softened
1   cup buttermilk
4   tablespoons honey
2   cups shredded Mexican cheese blend
2   cups your favorite chunky salsa
1   cup sour cream

PREHEAT OVEN TO 350 DEGREES. In a medium bowl, stir together cream cheese, garlic powder, seasoned salt, and corn; set aside. Place broken taco shells in a large Ziploc bag; seal bag and crush taco shells with a rolling pin until coarsely ground. Pour crumbs into a shallow dish; stir in chili powder. Place each chicken breast between pieces of waxed paper or plastic wrap, smooth side down, and gently pound with a flat side of a meat mallet or a rolling pin until breasts are about ¼-inch thick. Spread butter on one side of each chicken breast. Place about ⅓ cup of cream cheese mixture on center of buttered side of each chicken breast; roll up chicken. Pour buttermilk into a shallow dish. Dip chicken rolls in buttermilk, then dredge in crumb mixture. Use a toothpick to secure each chicken roll. Place chicken rolls in ungreased 9x13-inch glass baking dish. Drizzle with honey. Bake 35 to 45 minutes or until chicken is no longer pink in the center. Sprinkle with Mexican cheese blend; bake 5 more minutes to melt cheese. Serve with salsa and sour cream.

Serves 6 to 8.

CLASSIC CHEESE FONDUE

1   pound Velveeta® cheese
1   cup milk
1   teaspoon crushed garlic
     Salt and pepper, to taste
1   loaf French bread, cut into 1-inch cubes
     Assorted fruits and vegetables (broccoli, potatoes, cauliflower, carrots, grape tomatoes, sliced apples, sliced pears)

IN A 4-QUART SLOW COOKER, ADD CHEESE, milk, garlic, salt, and pepper. Melt cheese on low heat for 2 hours until smooth and creamy. Stir.

Arrange fruits and vegetables on a platter and, using forks or long skewers, dip individual pieces into the cheese.

Serves 6 to 8.

WEEK 50

This week, let the kids make simple, homemade butter. Shake a pint of heavy whipping cream until solid (about 5 minutes). Draw off excess liquid and open the carton. Put the sweet, creamy butter in a bowl and serve with the French Peasant Bread. Delicious!

BROCCOLI CHEESE SOUP

½   cup butter
1   sweet onion, finely chopped
4   cups chicken broth
1   16-ounce package frozen broccoli, or 2 pounds broccoli florets, washed and cut
2   cups cooked long-grain rice
1   cup heavy cream
3   cups cubed Velveeta® cheese
1   teaspoon seasoned salt
1   teaspoon dried basil

MELT BUTTER IN A LARGE SOUP POT OVER MEDIUM HEAT. Add onions and sauté until tender. Stir in chicken broth and broccoli. Bring to a boil. Reduce heat and simmer, uncovered, for 4 minutes. Add rice, cream, and cheese cubes. Cook on medium heat, stirring frequently, until cheese is fully melted and blended into a savory soup. Add seasoned salt and basil. Stir and serve.

Serves 6.

French Peasant Bread

1   package active dry yeast
2   cups warm water
1   tablespoon sugar
2   teaspoons salt
4   cups all-purpose flour
    Cornmeal, if needed
1   egg
1   tablespoon oatmeal
¼   cup butter, melted

Place yeast, water, and sugar in a warm bowl and stir until dissolved. Let stand 5 to 10 minutes. Add salt and stir. Add flour and stir until blended. Do not knead. Cover bowl with a kitchen towel and let rise one hour or until doubled in size. Flour hands, remove dough from the bowl and place in 2 rounds on a cooking stone or an oiled cookie sheet sprinkled with cornmeal. Let rise an additional hour. Beat the egg in a small bowl. With a pastry brush or fingers, brush the tops of the loaves of bread with egg and sprinkle the oatmeal on top. Bake at 425 degrees for 10 minutes. Reduce oven temperature to 375 degrees and cook an additional 15 minutes. Remove from the oven and brush again, this time with melted butter. Serve warm. You can tear pieces and dip in soup or you can slice it and serve with honey and butter.

Serves 6.

WEEK 51

This week, try this exciting new dish that will surely spice up your meals and light up your mood. The refreshing blend of mango and cilantro can give you the zip you need to put a smile on your children's faces.

BEAUTIFUL CHICKEN SALAD IN TORTILLA BOWLS

8   10-inch flour tortillas
1   teaspoon cumin
1   teaspoon salt
8   cups cooked, cubed chicken
3   cups cubed, peeled mango
3   tablespoons fresh lime juice
1   15-ounce can black beans, drained and rinsed
1   cup finely chopped tomato
1   cup fresh, chopped cilantro leaves
2   cups shredded iceberg lettuce
2   cups fresh spinach, chopped
1   teaspoon salt
1   recipe Mango Vinaigrette (see recipe on page 127)

PREHEAT OVEN TO 400 DEGREES. Cut 8 25x12-inch pieces of aluminum foil. Slightly crush each to form a 4-inch ball; flatten slightly. Place foil balls on ungreased cookie sheet. Spray one side of each tortilla with nonstick cooking spray. Sprinkle cumin and salt evenly over sprayed side of each tortilla. Gently shape each tortilla over a foil ball, placing seasoned side toward foil. Bake 5 to 7 minutes or until edges are golden brown. Let cool, leaving in pan and on foil until you are ready to use.

In large bowl, mix chicken and fresh mango. In a small bowl, mix lime juice and black beans. Add beans and remaining salad ingredients to chicken mixture. Divide mixture between taco bowls and drizzle with Mango Vinaigrette.

Serves 8.

MANGO VINAIGRETTE

1   cup cubed, peeled mango
½   cup mango nectar (from a 12.5-ounce can)
4   tablespoons white wine vinegar
2   tablespoons freshly squeezed lime juice
2   tablespoons freshly squeezed orange juice
2   tablespoons honey
⅔   cup olive oil

PLACE ALL INGREDIENTS EXCEPT OIL in the jar of a blender. Cover and process until smooth. With blender running, slowly pour oil through hole in top until mixture is thickened. Chill until ready to serve with a salad.

Vinaigrette will keep for 3 to 5 days.

Makes 2 cups.

WEEK 52

Kids tend to like rice and chicken. And after a whole year of trying new dishes, they should be open to trying something new, but with familiar ingredients such as chicken and rice. So, this week, tell the kids you're eating chicken and rice, but with a twist. Let them help you add the ingredients to the slow cooker, and be willing to omit items you know picky eaters will shun. Encourage kids to take at least one or two bites. The cashews add great texture to the main dish. I like to serve apple slices and caramel dip with this meal. And fortune cookies would make a really fun treat as well. To end the meal, you could slip your own homemade fortunes into store-bought fortune cookies. Include good wishes for the new year as part of the fortunes.

CHINESE CASHEW CHICKEN

2	cups sliced chicken
1	10.75-ounce can cream of mushroom soup
1	pound fresh bean sprouts
1	cup sliced celery
½	cup chopped green onions
1	8-ounce container fresh, sliced mushrooms
3	tablespoons butter
1	tablespoon soy sauce
1	teaspoon sesame oil
1	cup whole cashews
4 to 6	cups hot cooked rice

COMBINE CHICKEN, SOUP, BEAN SPROUTS, celery, onion, mushrooms, butter, soy sauce, and sesame oil in a 4-quart slow cooker. Mix well. Cover and cook on low for 4 to 6 hours or on high 3 to 4 hours. Stir in cashews just before serving. Serve over hot rice.

Serves 4 to 6.

ALMOND CHINESE CHEWS

3   eggs, lightly beaten
1   cup sugar
1   26-ounce jar or can almond filling
¼   teaspoon almond extract
¾   cup all-purpose flour
1   teaspoon baking powder
¼   teaspoon salt
   Powdered sugar

PREHEAT OVEN TO 300 DEGREES. Grease a 9x13-inch baking dish and set aside. In a medium bowl, beat eggs and sugar until thoroughly blended. Add almond filling and extract, beat until blended. In a separate bowl, mix together flour, baking powder, and salt; fold into almond mixture. Spread batter evenly in prepared pan. Bake 40 minutes or until wooden toothpick inserted in center comes out clean. Cool completely in pan on wire rack. Cut into 2-inch bars; dust with powdered sugar.

Makes about 2 dozen bars.

Index

ABOUT THE AUTHOR

Jill McKenzie's culinary education began at the feet of her parents and her incredible grandmother. Later, she cooked with friends and for neighborhood activities and events. Recipes have always interested her and she enjoys reading cookbooks as novels.

For thirteen years, Jill has enjoyed her career as a chef and professional cooking specialist. She has been a private chef, professional caterer, and taught cooking classes at women's expos, Utah Macey's grocery stores, and Utah Valley University, as well as private classes for in-home cooking and menu consultation. She also worked for a time as the *Daily Herald* chef.

Jill lives in Lehi, Utah, with her husband, Roger, and their six beautiful children. Besides cooking, her favorite things in life are her family, horses, science, people, and eating chocolate.